The laboratory mouse; its origin, heredity, and culture

Clyde E. 1900-1994 Keeler

Nabu Public Domain Reprints:

You are holding a reproduction of an original work published before 1923 that is in the public domain in the United States of America, and possibly other countries. You may freely copy and distribute this work as no entity (individual or corporate) has a copyright on the body of the work. This book may contain prior copyright references, and library stamps (as most of these works were scanned from library copies). These have been scanned and retained as part of the historical artifact.

This book may have occasional imperfections such as missing or blurred pages, poor pictures, errant marks, etc. that were either part of the original artifact, or were introduced by the scanning process. We believe this work is culturally important, and despite the imperfections, have elected to bring it back into print as part of our continuing commitment to the preservation of printed works worldwide. We appreciate your understanding of the imperfections in the preservation process, and hope you enjoy this valuable book.

STUDIES IN GENETICS

GENETICS AND EUGENICS

OUTLINES OF A LABORATORY COURSE
IN GENETICS

THE GENETICS OF DOMESTIC RABBITS

REPRINT OF THE ROYAL HORTICULTURAL
SOCIETY'S TRANSLATION OF MENDEL'S
PAPERS ON PLANT HYBRIDIZATION

HARVARD UNIVERSITY PRESS

CAMBRIDGE　　　　MASSACHUSETTS

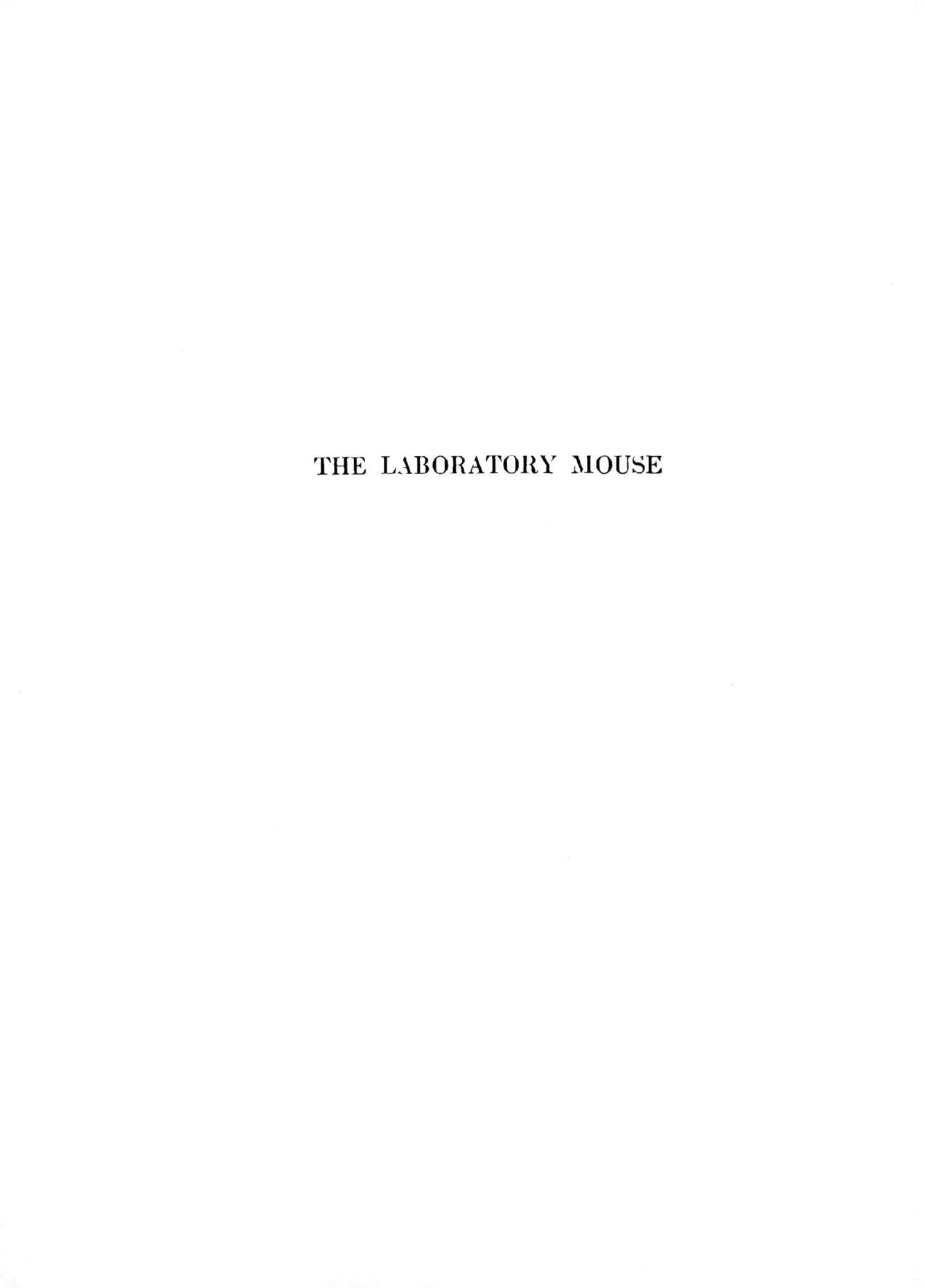

THE LABORATORY MOUSE

LONDON HUMPHREY MILFORD
OXFORD UNIVERSITY PRESS

THE LABORATORY MOUSE

ITS ORIGIN, HEREDITY, AND CULTURE

BY

CLYDE E. KEELER, Sc.D.
RESEARCH FELLOW OF THE HOWE LABORATORY
HARVARD MEDICAL SCHOOL
FELLOW BY COURTESY OF THE BUSSEY INSTITUTION

CAMBRIDGE

HARVARD UNIVERSITY PRESS

1931

COPYRIGHT, 1931
BY THE PRESIDENT AND FELLOWS OF HARVARD COLLEGE

PRINTED AT THE HARVARD UNIVERSITY PRESS
CAMBRIDGE, MASS., U.S.A.

CONTENTS

I	Introduction	3
II.	Geographical Distribution of the House Mouse	4
III	Antiquity of the Fancy Mouse	7
IV	Unit-Characters (Gene Mutations) of the House Mouse	19
V	Normal Inheritance	35
VI	Abnormal Inheritance	44
VII	The Breeding of Mice in Laboratories	47
Bibliography		73

37949

ILLUSTRATIONS

		PAGE
Fig. 1.	The Egyptian Cat-goddess, Bubastis	8
2.	Polychrome pottery mouse from Egypt	8
3.	A. A coin of Alexandria Troas bearing the cultus statue of Apollo Smintheus	10
	B. A coin of Tenedos (300 B.C.) bearing the statue of Apollo Smintheus and a mouse	10
4.	The Japanese God of Wealth, Dai-koku, and his symbolic white mouse	15
5.	The mouse netsuké by the Japanese artist, Masateru	19
6.	Diagram illustrating the inheritance of a simple, recessive, mendelizing unit-character such as albinism	36
7.	Diagram of a pair of chromosomes showing the linkage relationship of two pairs of genes before, during, and after a crossing-over	41
8.	Diagram of a back-cross illustrating the linkage between rodless retina and silver pelage	42
9.	Diagram of chromosomes of the house mouse with genes for unit characters distributed arbitrarily among them to show genetic independence or linkage of the characters	43
10.	Wire mouse cage used at the Bussey Institution	53
11.	Sectional view of feeding can	57
12.	Gray (wild coated)	59
13.	Brown extreme dilute ($bb\ c^d\ c^d$)	59
14.	Cinnamon chinchilla ($bb\ c^{ch}\ c^{ch}$)	59
15.	Albino (cc)	59
16.	Lethal yellow ($A^l\ A$)	61
17.	Non-agouti black (aa)	61
18.	Sooty yellow (sable) ($A^l\ a$)	61
19.	Black-and-tan or white-bellied non-agouti black ($at\ at$)	61
20.	Gray recessive spotted (piebald) (ss)	63
21.	Non-agouti black with dominant spotting ($aa\ Ww$)	63
22.	Japanese waltzer non-agouti black piebald (selected for whiteness) ($aa\ ss\ vv$)	63
23.	Non-agouti black-eyed-white (homozygous for piebald) ($aa\ Wu\ ss$)	63
24.	Blue or non-agouti dilute black ($aa\ dd$)	65
25.	Non-agouti silver ($aa\ ss$)	65
26.	Non-agouti brown ($aa\ bb$)	65

ILLUSTRATIONS

		PAGE
FIG 27	Short-ear lilac or pink-eye non-agouti black short-ear (*aa pp se se*)	65
28	Heterozygous naked ("nakt") (*Nn*)	67
29	Recessive hairless (*hr hr*)	67
30	Homozygous naked (*NN*)	67
31	Non-agouti dilute brown (*aa bb dd*) having developed two large transplanted tumors	67
32	New-born mouse showing posterior reduplication. (Courtesy of Dr C H Danforth)	69
33	Non-agouti silver, normal and dwarf (2 1–2 months old (*aa sl sl*) and (*aa sl sl dw dw*)	69
34	Albino showing flexed tail	69
35	Skulls of mice showing normal and parted frontals	69
36	Normal and rodless (*rr*) retinæ of the house mouse	69

THE LABORATORY MOUSE

I
INTRODUCTION

SMALL rodents will always find a place in the laboratory of the zoology teacher, the biological investigator, the medical researcher, and the fancier Each man has different problems in mind: behavior, physiology, disease, and beauty among others

On account of certain innate qualities the house mouse, *Mus musculus*, has become in many ways the laboratory mammal most favorable for culturing Its fertility, prolificity, convenient size, short gestation period, its manifold variations, inexpensive maintenance, resistance to open infections, susceptibility to certain diseases, and ease of production conspire to make it the laboratory animal par excellence The teacher of zoology uses variations of the house mouse to demonstrate the laws of heredity, the biological investigator employs them for physiological and genetic studies, the advanced medical man uses them as media in which to culture disease germs or for pathological tests as in the production of sera, and the fancier prizes them for their æsthetic appeal

Literature upon the house mouse, its origin, history, distribution, development, the nature of its variations, the hereditary transmission of its varietal characters, and methods of rearing it suitable for the needs of laboratories, has not been assembled so far as I am aware. The data are in some instances rare, usually widely scattered, and often inaccessible to those who could advantageously employ them Some are recorded in difficult and highly technical language Some of the data have never been published

To collect such valuable information as this concerning the house mouse and to present it in a usable form is the task of this book

II

GEOGRAPHICAL DISTRIBUTION OF THE HOUSE MOUSE

THE great order of Rodents or gnawing mammals is very successful as judged by the extent of its distribution and the degree of its adaptation to varied environments. Cavies scuttle under brush, rats slink about human habitations, mice squeeze through inconceivably small holes, squirrels scurry up trees and leap or glide from branch to branch, rabbits tunnel the earth, amphibious beavers fell trees and build dams. Yet all are hopelessly dependent upon their chisel-like incisors, which proclaim a common relationship and give them a common name.

The five families of rodents enjoying the widest distribution (7)[1] are the Leporidæ (rabbits, hares), the Hystricidæ (porcupines), Sciuridæ (squirrels), Cricetidæ (New World mice, meadow mice, hamsters), and the Muridæ (Old World rats and mice having tubercular teeth).

Because the rabbits have four incisors in the upper jaw and two in the lower, they have been assigned to the sub-order Duplicidentata (duplex-toothed) or even made a separate order, Lagomorpha. The porcupines, squirrels, rats, and mice bear two incisors both above and below and are placed in the sub-order Simplicidentata (simple-toothed).

Of these successful families the last two have attained world distribution, while the other three had established themselves before modern times in all geographical regions except the Australian.

The accepted classification of the common house mouse is

    Order Rodentia (gnawing animals)
      Sub-order Simplicidentata (simple-toothed)
        Family Muridæ (mouse-like animals)
          Genus Mus (true mice)
            Species musculus (the little mouse)

[1] Italic figures in parentheses refer to names listed numerically in the Bibliography at the end of the text.

The ancestral house mouse, from the present-day species of which the main breeds of the fancy are derived, is undoubtedly of Central Asiatic origin. The date of its first appearance in Eocene times and its subsequent expansion may only be conjectured in terms of numerous millennia. From the region of its early development it made its way to the habitable portions of Europe, Asia, and northern Africa, perhaps often as a stowaway in early human migrations. At the present time the species *Mus musculus* is represented in the old world by several interbreeding species and their natural varieties. In northern Africa and Syria the pale, white-bellied *M. musculus gentilis* is found. *M. musculus* of southeastern Europe is in general darker than that of northern Europe, and it seems to be the darker animal that became established in Mexico and South America through colonization by South Europeans, whereas the lighter form is more common in the United States and Canada.

The Asiatic *Mus bactrianus* group is lighter and more delicate than the European *M. musculus*, but breeds freely with it. Fancy breeds of mice often partake of blood of both types, while the Japanese waltzing mouse of the fancy may be derived (*158*, *59*) solely from the *bactrianus* of China or Tibet.

Mus bactrianus (or *wagneri* (*55*)) ranges from Persia to China. The general type of *bactrianus* blends into the short-tailed *M. bactrianus gansuensis* of Mongolia and into the long-tailed *M. bactrianus kakhyenensis* in Indo-China and the Malay peninsula (*4*).

The species *Mus musculus* proper shared with the European his recent conquest of the globe, and was unintentionally transported on ships or among merchandise to all habitable regions including the Asiatic seacoast normally within the range of the *bactrianus* group.

This internationalization of the mouse has been so recent, and complete isolation has been so rare, that few distinct varieties have been able to develop and persist as such in nature. However, where some isolation has been afforded, several color varieties have maintained themselves distinct for many years. For example, a white-bellied colony of mice has been found near Woods Hole, Massachusetts (*134*), in a region in northern France the black (non-agouti) form has become the sole house mouse to the exclusion of the normal gray variety; the Isle of Wight off the coast of England is populated with the pink-eyed variation

The present universal supremacy of *M. musculus* or *M. bactrianus* as house mouse is challenged only in very circumscribed localities where the white-footed field mouse occasionally supplants it The largest such area is thought to be southern Persia, where *Apodemus sylvaticus* takes its place

III

ANTIQUITY OF THE FANCY MOUSE

VARIATIONS of the word "mouse" found today in many European languages go back through the Latin *mus* and Greek *mus* or *mys* to *mush* in Sanscrit (*100*), the mother tongue of the race In Sanscrit *mush* is derived from a verb meaning "to steal" This suggests that man was well acquainted with the mouse and its predatory habits before the separation of the Aryan tribes in Asia some four thousand years before Christ One of the old Zoroastrian legends says that the moon chases away the clouds as a cat (weasel?) chases mice.

Rats and mice abounded in the ancient world from earliest times, especially where grain was stored. There are numerous historical accounts of excessive increase of these rodents constituting veritable plagues in ancient civilizations, sometimes accompanied by disease (*138*)

Stories of rats and mice became early incorporated in the folklore of the ancient world along with anecdotes about their enemies the cat and the weasel A specific word for house mouse as well as legends concerning it exist today in nearly every human dialect

In Egypt The fact that rats and mice appear so rarely in Egyptian art is probably due to the fact that they were considered undesirable animals, and for this same reason the Nubian cat, as a destroyer of rats and mice, was deified before the Third Dynasty (c. 2800 B.C.).

The sacred cat Bubastis (see Fig. 1) was not only the patron goddess of the prosperous delta city of Bast, but also the goddess of love and feminine fashion Iphthimis her son was the god of goodness In the holy city of Bast stood the famous cat mausoleum, where the remains of sacred felines were ceremoniously laid to rest in bronze or wooden cat-shaped coffins. Each year Lower Egypt thronged to the riotous feast of Bubastis, and families went through a mourning ritual for their deceased cats similar to that for human members of the household. Since the cat embodied all godly virtue, the mouse probably came to symbolize evil by contrast. Indeed, it may be suggested that rats and mice were probably responsible to a great degree for the cat's deification, because the Nile delta has been a grain-growing region since prehistoric times, and was undoubtedly overrun with these rodents before the advent of the cat from Nubia.

A glazed polychrome effigy of a white-bellied agouti mouse made in Egypt 2000 B.C. is in the British Museum (see Fig. 2).

A satyrical papyrus of the New Kingdom (*153*) (written between 1580–1205 B.C.) bears the picture of a rat or mouse (possibly *Mus alexandrinus*) in kingly robes, attended by Egyptian cats.

FIG. 1. The Egyptian Cat-goddess, Bubastis, redrawn from Keller after Perrot-Chipiez.

Aelianus (c. A.D. 100) remarks that in Lower Egypt mice develop from raindrops. St. Basil (A.D. 330–379) repeats the story of pluvial generation of mice in Egypt, but adds grasshoppers and frogs as co-creations.

FIG. 2. Polychrome pottery mouse from Egypt, c. 2000 B.C. (In British Museum.)

In Palestine. Moses received his cultural training in Egypt and with it the traditional hatred for mice. This attitude is exemplified among the commandments to the Hebrews recorded in the Book of Leviticus:

These also shall be an abomination to you among the creeping things that creep upon the earth, the weasel, and the mouse, and the tortoise after his kind.... These are unclean to you among all that creep whosoever doth touch them, when they be dead, shall be unclean until even

In the Old Testament is an account of a rat or mouse plague accompanied by intestinal disease which was brought upon the Philistines about 1000 B C following the seizure of the Israelitish "ark of the covenant." Golden effigies both of mice and of the affected portions of the human anatomy were given as gifts to Yahweh in order to appease his wrath [1]

In Asia Minor Probably the first recorded instance of the raising and protection of mice by men is in connection with the ancient mouse worship of Pontis instituted perhaps some fourteen hundred years before Christ Homeric legend (c 1200 B c) mentions *Apollo Smintheus* (god of mice) This cult was popular at the time of Alexander the Great (300 B C.)

During the latter part of the second millennium before Christ, Cretan Teucri invaders landed upon the shore of Asia Minor for the purpose of colonization For a long time they were restricted to the coast by the aboriginal Pontians, with whom they continuously contested in arms A decisive victory for the Cretans was credited to the mice (probably field mice), which their Apollo caused to gnaw the leather straps from the shields of the enemy (65).

Several Greek and Roman historians (*1, 163*) describe in some detail the temple which the conquering Teucri erected upon the Pontic island of Tenedos in gratitude to Apollo, god of mice Tradition has it that before the Teucri set out from Crete they had been given an oracle commanding them that where they settled there they should build a temple

---

[1] Herakles Kornopion, the Tyrian Sun god as well as Baalzebub (harmonized by the Greeks as the Fly god Zeus) frequently bears the mouse symbol. On a Carthaginian votive stone described by Vigouroux-Ibach are carved two mice as gifts to either Baal or Astarte-Aphrodite Herodotus says that the statue of Seti III within the temple of Ptah at Memphis had a mouse on the hand and bore the inscription "Look on me and be just!" (*100*)

to Apollo and worship the "earthborn creatures." The foundation of this temple was still standing in 1902. The accounts picture vividly a magnificent marble shrine overrun with sacred mice which were raised at public expense. They describe the altar, tripod, and statue of "Apollo, God of Mice." He stands stiffly in the style of the archaic Greek period. In his right hand he holds a patera, in his left he

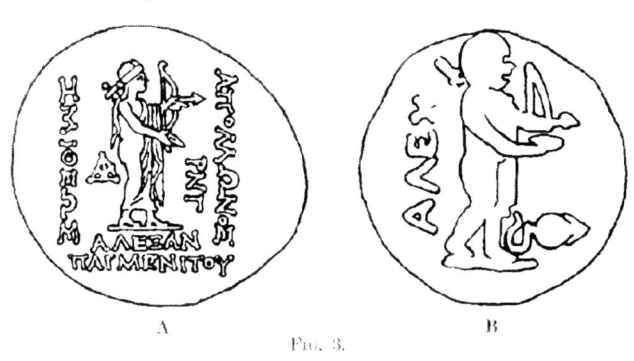

FIG. 3.

A. A coin of Alexandria Troas bearing the cultus statue of Apollo Smintheus. (Natural size.)
B. A coin of Tenedos (500 B.C.) bearing the statue of Apollo Smintheus and a mouse. (Enlarged about 3 diameters.)

carries a bow. At his feet is the huge effigy of a mouse, while a family of *white mice* have their nest under the altar itself (see Fig. 3).

A priestess of this temple, Herophila by name, was said to have correctly interpreted Queen Hecuba's dream concerning the fall of Troy and the fate of herself and family.

The mouse cult (*56, 169*) spread from Tenedos to Alexandria, Hamaxitus, Larissaia, Parion, Heraclea, Grynaeus, and Chryse in Asia Minor, and the god was even honored in Lesbian Arisba, Methymna, and Magnesia. Record of the cult is to be found in Athens and Thespia on the Greek mainland. In some of these centers it probably continued as a local form of worship until the Turkish conquest in 1453. Thus the Sminthian worship existed for about three thousand years and white mice were cultured in the temples for about two thirds of this period, mainly for auguries.[1]

[1] Jamblichos is authority for the statement that mice were employed for auguries in Babylon, while Aelianus mentions the soothsaying rites of Apollo Smintheus (*169*).

Coins of the Troad, and especially Alexandria Troas, frequently bear the figure of the cultus statue and in several instances the sacred mouse (*41*).[1]

Aristotle refers to the white mice of Pontis. Strabo (c. 25 B C) (*163*) mentions the white mice cultured in the many Sminthian temples. Pliny (c A.D 25) (*150*) alludes to the use of white mice for auguries White mice are mentioned by Aelianus (A D 100) (*1*), Hesychius (c A D. 500) (*100*), Suida (1100) (*65*), Albert (1250) (*65*), Apostolius (1453) (*65*), Gesner (1560) (*65*), Johnson (1640) (*84*), Pallas (1766) (*143*), and Darwin (1865) (*36*), while more recently the authorities writing upon them have been too numerous to mention

Pliny says in this connection

And verily how basely men thinke of this kind of cattell and hold them no better than vermine, yet are they not without certaine naturall properties, and those not to be despised but principally in regard of the sympathy between them and the planets in their ascent, I have noted heretofore and namely, considering how the lobes and filaments of their livers and bowels do increase or decrease in number according to the daies of the Moon's age By the learning of soothsayers, observed it is, that if there be a store of white ones bred it is a good signe and presageth prosperitie — Translation of Philemon Holland, 1635

The pharmaceutical virtues of the mouse so often employed by Greek and Christian doctors may be attributable in part to the influence of the mouse cult of Pontis

Greece and Rome. The Homeric story of "Batrachomyomachia" or the "Battle of Frogs and Mice" probably originated in Ionia about 750 B C An analagous story was popular in Europe during the early Christian centuries The latter tale was known as Galliomyomachia ("The Battle of Weasels and Mice"), and describes a war waged by the weasels upon the rats. The story may have been occasioned by the influx into Europe of the black rat (*Rattus rattus*) following the migration of the Germanic tribes, which animal finally gained a foothold in England during the fifteenth century.

[1] Coins of Nesos, Lampsakos, Nagidos, and Metapont bear a mouse

Aristotle (300 B C) said that mice were generated spontaneously from filth in houses and in ships. Horace (65-8 B C) wrote the famous story of the Country Mouse that returned a visit to his cousin the Town Mouse. Pliny (A D 23-79) in his *Historia Naturalis* classified the different kinds of mice, calling the house mouse "musculus" (little mouse), which name it bears today in zoological taxonomy. Pliny also recorded that the ashes of a weasel sprinkled about the house will keep away mice. He stated that in Ionia mice are generated by the overflowing of the Meander River, even causing the inhabitants to flee from their dwellings. He told of the driving out of the entire population of the Isle of Gyarus by mice which proceeded to gnaw the gold, iron, and steel left behind.

Europe In Christian Europe mice and rats fell into disrepute, becoming the companions of witches and sorcerers. This was partly due to the attitude of the Church following the condemnation of these creatures by Moses.

The clergy of the Middle Ages never ceased to comment upon the voluptuous and libidinous habits of mice. Indeed, mice were frequently raised by curious churchmen in order to observe their wicked actions. Albert (65) records that the white ones are very lustful. In this statement he follows Diogenes. Gesner (65) says they are libidinous. Erasmus records their lust [1] Part of the European attitude may have been due to plagues and current legends originating in Greek mythology.[2]

Horace (65 B C) spoke of the mountains being in labor and bringing forth a "ridiculus mus," which is to this day a proverb of futile effort. Aelianus calls them "earthborn creatures."[3] About A D 1500 Erasmus collected together

[1] The mouse was often a symbol of delicacy or lust in Greek drama. In the British Museum is a bronze mouse from Icoma which holds over its face the mask of a Silen, a creature usually represented as a man having a horse's tail, and the symbol of lust in the worship of Dionysos.

[2] The ancient Persians and Bactrians held that mice were creations of the wicked god Ahriman.

[3] A Talmudic fable speaks of a mouse in the process of creation, the fore parts already flesh and the hinder parts still earth.

some eight hundred legends, a number of which were reputed to be the works of Aesop (c 620-560 B C.). According to Erasmus this brand of murine-generation story was originated by Aesop and copied by Porphyrion (A D. 233-304), who gives the following account (65).

> As once when wild and uncivilized men saw the earth to heave up and move in a mountain, they ran together from every direction to such a dreadful sight, expecting that the earth would there give forth some new and great spectacle (the mountain indisputably laboring) Perhaps it should be that the Titans would burst forth again and renew their war with the gods! Then, while all the multitude stood there in suspense with astonished spirits, a mouse broke out of the earth, and a laugh arose from all the people

Plutarch (A.D 46-120) says that mice conceive by licking salt. He copies this from Aristotle, who not only believes in the saline method of engendering but records a ridiculous litter size of one hundred and twenty young produced through this kind of parthenogenesis. This story was brought to Aristotle by a veteran of Alexander's military campaign in India, who apparently wished to impress the old naturalist with the marvels of that far-away land Thomas of Cantimpre (c A D 1228-1244) avers that the size of mouse livers waxes and wanes with the moon, but in this he repeats Pliny

These legends expanded to their greatest proportions during the Middle Ages when mice along with other base creatures were considered the handiwork of devils Casper Schott (A D 1697) (156) in his interesting *Physica Curiosa* is bold enough to suggest that diabolical assistance may not be necessary in the creation of lowly animals as commonly believed, because many of the forms are known to be produced by spontaneous generation He says

> The first reason for doubting is because many animals arise from putrid material and by other means without the intervention of father and mother Indeed, agile boring larvae and little worms are given birth in rotting wood, from putrefaction slugs, snails and mice, from ox dung honey bee drones and wasps, from the aerated urine of caterpillars, butterflies, ants, grasshoppers, cicadas and other similar forms

In this tale he follows Pliny, who in turn copies it from Aristotle.

The reputed parthenogenetic reproduction of the mouse was held up by the clergy as an example of the naturalness of human parthenogenesis demanded by Christian theology

Before the advent of the Persian cat into northern Europe during the time of Charlemagne, mice and rats frequently multiplied in such numbers that they could not be kept in check by the weasels maintained by the more fortunate families These conditions gave rise to such stories as that of the Pied Piper of Hamlin

The early Greek and Roman physicians employed mice in their medicinal formulæ Hippocrates (300? B C) says that he did not test the virtue of mouse blood as a cure for warts, prescribed by his colleagues, because he had a magic stone with lumps upon it which had proved an efficient remedy Galen (A D 130?–200?) advocates equal parts of mouse blood, cock s gall, and woman's milk mixed and dried as a cure for cataract Villanova uses dog's urine and mouse blood for warts.

During the Dark Ages the formulæ became increasingly occult and complicated, and mice figured even more in the pharmacopœia [1] St Hildegarde of Bingen (1098–1179) recounts that mice are a cure for epilepsy The manuscript known under the name of *Picatrix* (1256) endorses fumigation with fourteen bats and twenty-four mice Peter of Albano employs mouse dung as a cure for poisons, probably influenced by Pliny's freshly killed mouse poultice for serpent bites [2]

---

[1] The mouse seems to disappear from medical formulæ during the latter part of the seventeenth century, although crab claws and millipeds persist even in the literature of the last century The London Pharmacopœia (*164*) of 1667 instructs as follows "A flead mouse dried and beaten to powder, and given at a time, helps such as cannot hold their water or have Diabetes, if you do the like three daies together" The influence of this dictum was felt at Boston, Massachusetts, as late as 1890, when a family of English extraction fed mouse stew to their children to prevent bed-wetting

[2] In Europe mice used to be eaten as a remedy for toothache New-born mice dissolved in olive oil are a popular panacea for human ills in Turkey and Greece today.

ANTIQUITY OF THE FANCY MOUSE

The Orient. Although until recently the house mouse has been openly despised by Christian teachers, in the Orient, on the contrary, it has always enjoyed a much higher social rating.

Albino mice were used by the Chinese priests for auguries and during many centuries the government preserved records of their taking in the wild. These records cover the period

FIG. 4. The Japanese God of Wealth, Daï-koku, and his symbolic white mouse. (After a print in the Museum of Fine Arts in Boston.)

between A.D. 307 and A.D. 1641. During this time the finding of about thirty albino mice was recorded by the magistrates.

From Turkestan to Japan, years are reckoned in cycles of twelve, the first year of each cycle being named the "Mouse."

In Japan the mouse of the folk-sagas is a very wise creature and the symbol and messenger of the God of Wealth, Daï-koku (see Fig. 4). The god is usually represented as standing upon two sacks of rice with a mouse perched at his feet. The time between 11 P.M. and 1 A.M. is known as the hour of the mouse. A children's story describes the wedding of the mice.[1] Thus national tradition provided a psychological attitude among the Japanese most favorable for the development of the mouse as a fancy animal. In Japan today the mouse fancy is well developed, having thriven for at least three centuries.

It is difficult to ascertain how long varieties of the house mouse have been recognized in China. The word for white mouse is ancient, and that for spotted mouse appears in the earliest Chinese lexicon, written 1100 B.C. The waltzing variety has been known since 80 B.C. That the Nipponese of Yokohama and elsewhere zealously collected new varieties in foreign lands is shown by the fact that they call a mouse bearing certain markings the "Nanking Mouse" (162), while the Chinese fanciers of Shanghai near Nanking deny its origination and call it the *foreign mouse*. The Japanese waltzer was undoubtedly derived, at least in part, from *Mus bactrianus (wagneri)* of Tibet, as pointed out by Bowdler Sharpe (158) in 1912. Moreover, *Mus musculus* proper is not native to Japan. Perhaps the Japanese procured the European *M. musculus* varieties from Portuguese traders.

The Japanese had in their fancy such varietal characteristics as albinism, non-agouti, chocolate, waltzing, dominant and recessive spotting, and possibly blue dilution, pink-eyed dilution, and lethal yellow.

Something over a hundred years ago several of these fancy varieties of the house mouse were taken from Japan to Europe by British traders, and only a few decades ago did muriculture spread to America.

During the nineteenth century a number of European zoologists bred fancy mice for scientific investigation of the inheritance of varietal characters. They accumulated valuable information, but the meaning of these data remained unknown until the rediscovery of Mendel's Law of Heredity in 1900 (33).

---

[1] The Japanese have a saying that white mice are good and honest while dark ones are wicked and dishonest. Believing that good overcomes evil, some Japanese bring white mice into their houses in order to drive out the wild gray ones.

The essential feature of this law is the fact that the characteristics which differentiate domestic varieties are inherited as units, capable of being combined in all possible ways through the agency of hybridization. Up to the present time about two dozen such unit-characters have been recorded for the house mouse. The more important of these appear to have been first recorded at dates approximately as follows:

Character	Date	Authority
	B C	
Dominant spotting	c 1100	Lh Yah
Albinism	300	Aristotle
Waltzing	80	Annals of Han Dynasty
	A D	
Pink-eye dilution	1640	Johnson
Black	1640	Johnson
Recessive spotting (piebald)	1766	Pallas
Chocolate	1843	Gray
Naked (dominant hairless)	1850	Gordon
Chinchilla	c 1890	Blake
Extreme dilution	c 1890	"An old fancier"
Yellow	1902	Cuénot
Blue	1903	Bateson
Short ears	1921	Lynch
Rodless	1924	Keeler
Recessive hairless	1926	Brooke
Shaker	1926	Lord and Gates
Hyperglycæmia	1926	Cammidge and Howard
Dwarf	1929	Snell

In accordance with our present ideas, each unit-character made its appearance as a sudden, discontinuous physical or chemical change in the germinal substance, which forms the basis of heredity. We call such changes mutations, and the material bodies in which these changes occur are called genes. We can demonstrate the existence of a gene only when, as a consequence of mutation, it occurs in two different alternative forms in different individuals of the same species. By crossing individuals which bear different allelomorphs of the same gene, we can show that transmission of the contrasted characters conforms with Mendel's Law

Each unit-character is borne in or determined by a different gene, and is independent in its transmission of every other gene, except such as lie in the same chromosome with itself, a complication resulting in genetic linkage, a phenomenon to be more fully discussed later

IV

UNIT-CHARACTERS (GENE MUTATIONS) OF THE HOUSE MOUSE

The Japanese, as already stated, must be given credit for the development of a number of varieties of domestic mice. An ivory netsuké or sash pendant in the Louvre (*155*) carved about 1790 by the Japanese artist Masateru depicts a family of fancy mice in natural color among which one may distinguish the unit-characters pink-eye, piebald, non-agouti, albinism, and waltzing (see Fig. 5). Similar netsukés were popular during the nineteenth century.

FIG. 5. The mouse netsuké by the Japanese artist, Masateru. (After a photograph by Schlumberger.)

We have reason to believe that each unit-character arose by mutation or physical change in a particular gene located in a particular chromosome of a germ cell, and that this condition was transmitted to subsequent generations through heredity, the character manifesting itself in those individuals which carried certain hereditary combinations.

We may also be confident that identical sports have arisen in the wild at different times in remote parts of the world. Among the stuffed skins of the house mouse in the British Museum collections in 1926 were found pink-eyed dilutes from the Isle of Wight off the coast of England and from Zanzibar (the same variety was recently taken in the wild in Germany). Albinos had been collected from numerous localities. Several pied mice were listed from Syria. Blue-dilute specimens came from Esthonia and Syria, non-agouti (black) specimens from Cape Colony and England. Cinnamons were taken in South Africa and the Tigris Valley. There were white-bellied agoutis from Syria and Persia. Several specimens from West Africa probably contained extreme dilution. The mice were all taken in the wild and not purchased from fanciers. These facts refute the common belief that the varietal characteristics found in fancy stocks are the results of domestication. The natural cause which produces such mutations in the germ cells is as yet undiscovered. Under laboratory conditions β-rays of radium and X-rays are able to produce in the fruit fly (*Drosophila*) mutations identical with those appearing in this species in nature (*139*). It is possible that cosmic rays in nature are responsible for the origin of some of the house-mouse variations.

Myriads of mutations may arise and be lost in nature without ever being seen by man. Where accidentally a mutation has struck the fancy of man, he has secured and propagated it in captivity, selecting in the following generations for the particular character in question. Where a mutant form arises in any one of the thousands of laboratories breeding mice today (*113, 71, 160, 146*), it is quite likely to come to the attention of man and be preserved. Thus the number of mutants recorded as found in the wild is not comparable with the number observed to have originated in laboratory stocks nor is it legitimate to conclude that the mutation rate in captivity is greater than that in the wild.

Gray (normal wild coat). The gray coat (*42*) of a wild house mouse (see Fig. 12) is produced by the deposition of two kinds of pigment (yellow and black) in different portions of the hairs. Yellow is present normally in an apical or subapical band of many of the hairs. In general upon the ventral pelage the band becomes wider and the black pigment less, giving the belly a distinctly lighter appearance than the back. These pigment differences may be due to different types and rates of pigment production in the hair follicle, with an inhibitor for the black process when the banded region is forming. Chocolate pigmentation which takes the place of black in some fancy varieties may be looked upon as a condition in which the black reaction has been checked in an early phase.

Albinism (c, mutant form of the color gene, C)

The white mouse of Pontis is said to ruminate.—Aristotle, 300 B.C.

Complete albinism (see Fig. 15) is a condition in which pigmentation is entirely wanting in all parts of the body. Not only are external organs devoid of pigment but even those internal regions which normally develop pigment, such as the eyeball and the outer surfaces of the brain and spinal cord, are unpigmented. Animals bearing albinism have white hair and pink skin. The eye color is usually either pink or whitish according to whether or not the retinal blood supply is visible through the iris. Histological examination reveals the fact that in albinos pigment granules are present which are normal in shape and distribution, but which are leucotic.

A common explanation (140) for the production of albinism is the absence of the colorless tyrosinase, which ferment, working upon the base or substrate, tyrosin, converts it into the pigment melanin. Several chemical reactions are involved in the process. Some maintain that it is the tyrosin which is lacking in albinos. This assumption appears more probable in view of the allelomorphic series of dilutions produced by different forms of the albino gene.

The gene or hereditary determiner for albinism in the mouse is the lowest step in a series of alternative chemical states possible for this particular gene. The other states of this gene produce respectively normal pigmentation (C), chinchilla (c^{ch}), and extreme (Himalayan) dilution (c^H). A corresponding complete series of allelomorphs is found in rabbits. Albinism in crosses (18, 69) behaves as a recessive to normal pigmentation, chinchilla (*157*), and extreme dilution (*39*).

Complete albinism or one of its allelomorphs in which very little pigment is produced is known to occur in fish, birds, and most species of mammals, including man

Extreme Dilution (c^H)

Mr J E Knight brought into my laboratory a young male mutant mouse which he had captured in a corn crib. This animal gave the appearance of being an ordinary black eyed white in which the hair was apparently very slightly stained or dirty — Detlefsen, 1921

The above description of the extreme-dilute mouse (see Fig 13) is quite accurate (*39*). These animals vary in shade but are always a dirty white color. This is apparently due to a complete suppression of yellow and an almost complete suppression of black and brown in the coat. I have found that intense pigmentation persists in the ears, eyes, upon the tail, and to a lesser degree upon the feet.

In the possession of pigmented extremities this mutant resembles Himalayan albinism of the rabbit, and indeed its determiner occupies a corresponding position among the alternative forms of the albino gene

Upon superficial examination of extreme dilutes it is impossible to distinguish blacks, browns, agoutis, non-agoutis, and so forth. Closer inspection and continued handling enables one to differentiate blacks from browns by the shade of pigment upon the ears. These distinctions may be confirmed by clearing the iridæ in xylol. Such prepared iridæ show normal black or chocolate pigmentation according to whether the animal is genetically a black or a brown [1]

Chinchilla (c^{ch})

Thus the first generation of hybrids (between wild gray house mice and fancy albinos) consisted of 342 mice, of which 329 were gray, seven yellow and six chinchillas. — Schuster, 1905

[1] An old fancier in the fourth edition of *Fancy Mice* says: "Occasionally impure breeds and strains (of albinos) are raised in which there are black ears, eyes, and feet." This may indicate extreme dilution, which being a dominant allelomorph to true albinism might carry it as a recessive and continue to produce true albinos generation after generation

The chinchilla mouse with black agouti coat may be described (157) as a bluish gray containing no yellow, its pelage resembling closely that of the gray squirrel Brown agouti animals containing the chinchilla factor (see Fig 14) are easily distinguished by their brownish coat, with white rather than yellow bands of the agouti distribution pattern

Chinchilla has a tendency to remove yellow from the coat, although it also dilutes black and brown pigments, changing non-agouti black to sepia This leaves parts of agouti hairs almost white and the bellies of agouti chinchilla animals are usually quite colorless.

The yellow-reducing tendency is easily demonstrated by the fact that when lethal-yellow mice are crossed with chinchillas and yellow animals are produced carrying two doses of chinchilla, these animals have a cream coat and black eyes

Chinchilla (157, 57) of the mouse corresponds to chinchilla of the rabbit both in appearance and genetic behavior, being in both cases produced by a form of the albino gene recessive to normal pigmentation and dominant to both extreme dilution (Himalayan) and true albinism [1]

Pink-eyed dilution (p)

Scaliger saw another (mouse) very bright, with flaming eyes — Johnson, 1640

This mutation (see Fig. 27) reduces greatly the black or brown pigment, giving the eye a beautiful pink tint, from the color of the blood in the eyeball The coat of the agouti black is changed to a fawn. The coat of the agouti brown (cinnamon) becomes also a fawn but more brilliant than the pink-eyed black agouti, because brown pigment replaces

---

[1] Dr C Carter Blake (*Fancy Mice*, fourth edition) in a letter written about 1890 describes two crosses in which albinos mated with albinos produced colored young His results may be explained if it be assumed that the male used was really a synthetic albino homozygous for pink-eye, heterozygous for non-agouti, brown, and spotting, and bearing one dose each of chinchilla and albinism If this be the true explanation of these crosses, then human experience with chinchilla antedates Schuster's crosses in which chinchilla came in heterozygously from a gray mouse caught in the wild

black Pink-eyed dilution (*32, 23, 19, 54*) changes non-agouti black to "lilac" and transforms chocolate to "café au lait"

That pink-eyed dilution works only upon black and brown pigment is demonstrated by the fact that the coat color of lethal yellow is almost unchanged by the addition of pink-eyed dilution although the black eye of the lethal yellow is changed to pink.

Non-agouti (a)

As to color, many are like the ass; however some are cinerous, others even black, others from brown to red. — Johnson, 1640

Non-agouti (see Fig 17) is due to a mutation resulting in loss from the individual hairs of the normal banded distribution pattern determined by the gene A. No yellow apical band is formed in the non-agouti animal, but the black or brown pigment extends the full length of the hair Absence or inactivation of the agouti gene (A) in the mutant type non-agouti (*53 54*) (aa), changes a gray mouse to black and a cinnamon to rich chocolate.

Lethal yellow (A^Y)

In my cultures I found in addition yellow mice — Cuénot, 1902

Presence of the yellow mutation (see Fig 16) in a mouse is easily recognized by its brilliant yellow coat and jet-black (or brown) eye. These effects are due to the complete or nearly complete suppression of black pigment, save in the eye In the eye of a yellow mouse black pigment is even more abundant than in that of a black mouse, as proven by clearing specimens of both types in xylol.

Yellow is a dominant character, i e it requires but one dose of the gene to cause the animal to exhibit the character Animals containing two doses of the yellow gene (homozygotes) are inviable (*15, 24, 104, 20, 79*). Thus, as the yellow gene is an allelomorph to the agouti (*166*) (A) and non-agouti (a) genes, a yellow mouse will contain one dose of yellow and one of either agouti or non-agouti ($A^Y A$ or $A^Y a$).

Those yellows which contain a non-agouti gene (*a*) are often sooty yellow (see Fig 18) in appearance, and have sometimes been called "sables" (*47, 54*)

Chocolate yellows are clearer in color than those containing black, i e. have a less sooty appearance

Reds ($A^Y A$, or $Y^1 a$ plus darkening modifiers)

These animals of the fancy are a dull red, similar in color to Rhode Island Red fowls

Genetically they are lethal yellows with intensifying modifiers. They breed as yellows, but the complete genetics of the modifiers has not yet been worked out, although Dunn (*46*) has studied it extensively and has shown that it must be considered as due to numerous modifying genes

Dominant spotting (W) (broken spotting)

A mouse with the hair pattern of a leopard — Eh Yah, c 1100 B C

This variety (see Fig 21) is characterized by the presence of small irregular broken spots or polka-dot patches of color upon a white ground In higher grades pigmentation persists about the eyes and dorso-caudal region only

Dominant spotting (*112, 162, 53, 72*) is expressed, as the name indicates, in animals containing but one dose of the gene Homozygotes die of anæmia at an early age, under eighteen days (*37, 40*). Fancy breeds of this type are known as black-eyed whites (see Fig 23). They contain one dominant-spotting gene and two recessive-piebald genes, i e. are heterozygous for dominant spotting and homozygous for recessive piebald In some strains, perhaps all, pure-breds (homozygotes) are inviable. Dominant spotting may be due to localized inhibitors for the tyrosin-tyrosinase reaction. This type of spotting has come to us from Japan. In Chinese history it is recorded that in 120 B C. (or more probably A.D 40) a wise court official who was able to recall the name of this variety was rewarded by the Emperor with a cartload of silken textiles.

Recessive spotting (s) ("piebald")

I have seen indeed a gray variety with a white saddle and also a white variety spotted with black. — Pallas, 1766

In this type (see Fig. 20), large unbroken areas of white are present upon the belly, back, and face (*3*). There is a tendency to form a white belt and a white face. Recessive spotting (*61*) in its highest grade usually leaves two patches of pigment about the ears, the rest of the coat being white. This is the condition usually found in the Japanese waltzing mouse (see Fig. 22). Additional pigmented spots when present are usually found upon the rump. Animals bearing but one dose of the higher grades of spotting often have a small belly patch of white, but are otherwise colored. It is possible by systematic selection to produce strains with white faces or belts (*50*). What has been said concerning the probable immediate cause of dominant spotting (tyrosintyrosinase inhibition) applies to recessive spotting as well.

Yellow belly (A^W, a^t) (white belly, light belly)

The back is a gray tinged with red-brown, the belly is bordered with red-brown, the exact livery of the field mouse. — Cuenot, 1907

It has been found in the laboratory as well as in the wild state that mice may mutate (*113, 136*) to a yellow-bellied or white-bellied condition (see Fig. 19), in which the ventral hairs have an exceedingly long, light, apical band, in some cases even to the exclusion of all other pigment. There is a characteristically sharp demarcation on the sides and under the chin, with a patch of darkly pigmented hair upon the neck, shaped like a bow tie.

This bodily distribution pattern behaves as a dominant to all known color characters or their combinations, including yellow, i.e. it may be associated with the general coat coloration of any other type. It has been found in agouti (*23, 137*) and non-agouti forms (*146*), but not in combination with the lethal-yellow mutation. The wild gray mouse possessing this character has a normal back and a white or buff belly often tinged with red-brown along the sides (A^W)

A black mouse bearing this pattern is known as black-and-tan (a^t) (*51*). The chocolate mouse with this pattern is a chocolate-and-buff. The genetic relations of A^W to a^t are uncertain, except that they behave as allelomorphs of each other and of the agouti gene A.

When a gray mouse is crossed with a black-and-tan, the offspring are light-bellied grays. Progeny of identical appearance may be produced when white-bellied grays are crossed with blacks. Black-and-tan and white-bellied gray have usually been regarded as two additional allelomorphs of the yellow, agouti, non-agouti series (*51, 23*). But it would seem to be a more probable explanation that white belly depends upon a gene closely linked with the agouti gene. This explanation eliminates the paradox of the black-and-tan, which, when crossed to gray, produces offspring in which the back behaves as a recessive and the belly as a dominant.

Brown (b)

The first definite record of the brown mouse is found in a specimen list of mammals in the British Museum by Gray, 1843.

The brown condition (see Fig. 26) is one in which black pigment throughout the coat, skin, and eyes is replaced by chocolate (*54, 110*). This is thought to be due to an early interruption of the reaction which regularly produces black pigment. The mouse which would otherwise be wild gray coated becomes a cinnamon when homozygous for the brown gene, and the unticked or non-agouti form becomes pure chocolate in color.

Blue dilution (d)

Blues may be thrown by blacks and then breed true — Bateson, 1903.

A gray mouse homozygous for blue dilution (*9*) has a coat exhibiting a washed-out appearance known as blue-gray (*53, 54, 72, 110*). A non-agouti black when homozygous for blue dilution (see Fig. 24) becomes lead colored like a Maltese cat. A chocolate mouse which is also dilute is of a "silver-fawn" color The blue-dilute condition consists in a reduction in number of pigment granules in addition to a clumping of these granules. There is no noticeable change in iris pigmentation, but the cleared retina is lighter in color than that of the normal black eye

Naked (N) (dominant hairless, "half-naked")

The whole bodies of these three little creatures were completely naked, as destitute of hair and as fair as a child's cheek There was nothing peculiar about the snout, whiskers, ears, lower half of the legs and tail all of which had hair of the usual length and colour — Gordon, 1850

Naked (see Fig 28) is a peculiar physiological condition of the skin causing alternate waves of falling hair and regeneration (66) These waves (108) pass from head to tail, three or four waves being visible at a given time Vibrissæ are present as well as the short hairs upon the tail The homozygous naked (see Fig. 30) is devoid of tail hair and vibrissæ, and is semi-lethal Animals of this constitution are difficult to raise and are usually sterile These mice have the skin normal in texture and general appearance The genetics of this variation as a dominant unit-character was first worked out by Lebedinsky and Dauvart (1927)

Recessive hairless (hr) (rhinocerus?) (151, 3, 14)

In November, 1924, I received from a gentleman in North London, a pair of pink, smooth-skinned, hairless mice, which he had captured in his aviary — Brooke, 1926

This type of hairless animal (see Fig 29) has no tail hair but retains vibrissæ (12, 130, 60) It has wrinkled, dry skin of at least three times normal thickness A few aberrant hairs coil about within and even under the skin Such hairs may be seen in the dried skin, which is rendered transparent by the natural oil contained within it. The skin is filled with granular cysts Hairless females are usually sterile and the stock is maintained by breeding hairless males to their heterozygous sisters The gene for hairless (hr) is linked with piebald (s)

Short ears (se)

The mutation was found in a stock which originally came from the Lathrop mouse farm and consists in a noticeable difference in size of ears — Lynch, 1921.

As the name would indicate, this variety is characterized by small ears (see Fig. 27) It is due to arrested development of the auditory pinna (127) When both short-eared and normal-eared animals are found in the same litter, one is often able to distinguish the classes upon the fourteenth day after birth

While the normal ear increases in length of pinna (87) during the time from the fourteenth to the twenty-eighth day from 0 71 to 1 16 cm (63 per cent increase), the short ear shows a gain from 60 to 76 cm (27 per cent increase). The skull shape of the short-eared mouse differs from that of normals in that the nose is broader, while the cranium is much narrower. The zygomatic arch is squarer than in the normal There is a certain amount of sterility noticeable among short-ear animals. The gene underlying the development of short ears is tightly linked with that for blue dilution and there is a relationship, not completely worked out, between short ears and wavy tail This latter relationship will be touched upon under the heading of wavy tail.

Wavy tail

The behavior of this mutation is, like tailless, eccentric — Gates, 1927.

Some mice from birth show in the tail a series of zigzag waves (61) bent in the horizontal plane Such a condition is commonly found in short-ear stocks Wavy tail is purely a neuromuscular condition (87), more extreme when the animal is excited and disappearing in sickness, death, or under anæsthesia. The loci of the flexures are constant throughout life, as may be shown by tattooing a spot at the point of each flexure. X-ray photographs reveal that the caudal vertebræ are unaffected The extended wavy tail is of normal length Snell maintains (159) that wavy tail is but a second expression of the short-ear gene Yet in some short-ear families wavy tail appears to be absent. In some long-ear stocks it is present. In the absence of complete genetic analysis it is impossible to say whether the short-ear stocks with straight tails lack the wavy tail through absence of a gene or merely through lack of muscle tonus. If the wavy tail is not another expression of the short-ear gene, then it is linked with short ears as the researches of Gates and Keeler have shown. The inheritance is probably that of a weakly dominant unit-character.

Flexed tail (f) (kinky?)

In all cases the tail is permanently rigid over a varying portion of its length, this stiffness being particularly conspicuous proximally. The rigidity may be accompanied by permanent V-shaped, U-shaped, spiral, etc., flexures. — Hunt and Permar, 1928

In some of the short-ear stocks bearing wavy tail a complete right-angle flexure is found (*11, 78, 148, 44*). The joint is solidified by the fusion of vertebræ and the presence of an osteosis. Sometimes two or three of these flexures may be present in the same tail. This character may or may not be that reported by Plate, 1910. Such heritable flexures are found in long-ear stocks, but the identity or relationship of these characters is uncertain. The inheritance of flexures has been described by Hunt and Permar as a recessive which sometimes fails to come to recognizable expression.

Danforth, (*27*), in speaking of kinky tail (see Fig. 34) says

In these the caudal intestine instead of completely degenerating after the sixteenth day as in normal individuals, persists until birth as small remnants which become cystic or granular. Above these cysts the developing cartilages are thrown out of alignment and finally ankylose with each other, forming permanent kinks.

Posterior reduplication

By selection there has been developed a strain of mice which give a high percentage of young showing varying degrees of posterior reduplication. — Danforth, 1930

This character (see Fig. 32) ranges from polydactyly to completely formed additional posterior parts including legs, genitalia, and alimentary tract (*27*). The inheritance of the character is recessive and approximates the behavior expected of a unit-character, with a deficiency probably due to its low viability

Waltzing (v)

In 80 B C   in the ninth moon, a yellow mouse was found dancing with its tail in its mouth in the gateway of the palace of the Kingdom of Yen [now the province of Chih] The animal danced incessantly The king asked the queen to feed it with wine and meat but this did not interfere with the performance The mouse died during the night — *Annals of the Han Dynasty* (translation by Quentin Pan)

Waltzing mice (see Fig. 22) are unable to orient themselves upon a horizontal plane, and this results in a rapid and erratic turning or whirling. Waltzers make many turning, twisting, and jerking head movements (*183*) Waltzers are totally deaf (*182*) Different investigators disagree as to whether or not the semicircular canals are morphologically normal. Waltzers are very delicate, poor mothers, and quite susceptible to cold. The most common inbred strain of Japanese waltzers in America is non-agouti black and bears a high grade of recessive piebald, with the anatomical characteristics of *Mus bactrianus (wagneri)*. Waltzing is inherited as a simple recessive (*25, 31, 32, 61, 76*)

Gates (*63*) bred a waltzer containing but one dose of waltzing, which presumably through a faulty cell division had lost that portion of the normal chromosome which contains the allelomorph of waltzing Painter's histological investigation (*142*) confirmed this conclusion

Shaker (sh)

The mutation shows itself principally in the form of nervous head movements — Lord and Gates, 1928

The shaker (*126*) makes choreic head movements similar to those of the waltzer but lacks the circling movements. The character is recessive and linked with albinism and pink-eyed dilution

Rodless retina (r)

Microscopic sections of these eyes showed the total absence of visual cells (rods) — Keeler, 1924

This retinal defect (see Fig. 36) is characterized by complete absence of rod and external molecular layers and a great reduction of the cell number in the external nuclear layer (*86, 90*). The condition is readily detected by examining histological sections of the retina. The iris of the rodless eye contracts (*88, 89*) upon exposure to light and the blindness of rodless mice may be detected only by precise and carefully conducted animal-behavior tests (*87*). Rodless eyes secrete no visual purple (*90*) and produce no electric action current responses (*99*) to stimulation by light. The recessive gene producing rodless retina is linked (*98*) with that producing silver.

Dwarf (dw)

In the case of dwarf mice, mature individuals are only about one-fourth the weight of their normal brothers and sisters, scarcely bigger, in fact, than the ordinary mouse 16 or 17 days old. — Snell, 1929

These creatures (see Fig. 33) are probably pituitary-deficient dwarfs[1] The character is determined by a recessive gene (*160*).

Hyperglycæmia (hy)

The findings obtained with the second generation confirmed the conclusion that hyperglycæmia, like albinism, is a recessive character. — Cammidge and Howard, 1926

It has been definitely established (*13*) that a certain strain of mice bear a gene, which in the homozygous state raises the fasting blood-sugar proportions. Whereas normal mice have a blood-sugar content of 74–84 mg per 100 cc of blood, the mutant strain bears from 113–124 mg per 100 cc. The factor concerned is not linked with albinism but further genetic analysis is wanting.

Other characters Numerous other mouse variations are known to breeders of mice. Some of these characters are

---

[1] A paper by P. E. Smith and E. C. MacDowell in the Anatomical Record, vol 46, p 249, published too late for inclusion in the bibliography, confirms that the dwarfed condition is due to anterior pituitary deficiency and may be corrected by injection of rat pituitary.

erratic in their appearance and may depend upon several factors, genetic or environmental. Hagedoorn reported a genetic modifier of blue dilution (*72*). Heterozygosity for brown, pink-eye dilution, or albinism also has a tendency to lighten the coat. Little and Tyzzer (*122*) believe that susceptibility to development of a certain sarcoma found in the Japanese waltzing mouse is dependent upon three or four independently inherited Mendelizing factors. The evidence is derived from a cross between Japanese waltzing mice and ordinary fancy mice in which the first generation was susceptible but in the second generation there appeared a certain percentage of mice of non-susceptible constitution. Other tumor susceptibilities (see Fig 31) have been demonstrated to be hereditary (*121, 43, 124, 165*).

Several times in recent years a black-silver strain of mice has thrown occasional individuals bearing a symmetrical lacing pattern of white hairs. Its genetics is complex. Congenital cataract and stationary pupils have been found to run in certain mouse families. A dilution effective in combination with pink-eyed black was found several years ago, but has not been completely analyzed. Recently a separation of the metopic suture, parted frontals (see Fig 35), was reported (*97*) as a dominant unit-character. A twisted condition of the nasal bones behaving irregularly in heredity was also found (*96*).

Another strain of mice produces individuals lacking kidneys (*6*), or having lesions of the eyes, head, or feet (*120*). These are probably related, or expressions of the same process determined by the same genetic factors.

Nomenclature. The compound breeds of the house mouse are merely combinations of the simple characters already described. It is customary in scientific circles to designate the breeds by analytical names, but the fancier and layman often employ other terms, usually descriptive. In the following list are given the more common fancier's terms and their analytical equivalents followed by their genetic formulæ in terms of mutated genes.

Fancier's Term	Scientific Term	Genetic Formula
Gray	Gray agouti, wild	No mutations
Black	Non-agouti	aa
Cinnamon	Brown agouti	bb
Chocolate	Non-agouti brown	$aa\ bb$
Fawn with pink eyes	Pink-eye agouti	pp
Clear fawn with pink eyes	Pink-eye brown agouti	$bb\ pp$
Lilac, blue-lilac	Pink-eye non-agouti	$pp\ aa$
Champagne, café au lait	Pink-eye non-agouti brown	$pp\ aa\ bb$
Blue, maltese	Dilute non-agouti	$dd\ aa$
Silver-fawn	Dilute non-agouti brown	$dd\ aa\ bb$
Pearl	Pink-eye dilute non-agouti	$pp\ dd\ aa$
Silver-champagne	Pink-eye dilute brown non-agouti	$pp\ dd\ bb\ aa$
Yellow	Yellow, lethal yellow	$A^y A$
Sooty, sable	Sooty, sable (one of the expressions of lethal yellow often carrying non-agouti)	$A^y a$
Cream, light yellow	Dilute yellow	$dd\ A^y A$
Pied, piebald, Dutch spotted	Recessive spotting	ss
Variegated	Dominant spotting	Ww
Black-eyed white	Black-eyed white	$Ww\ ss$
Black-and-tan	Yellow-belly non-agouti	$aa^t,\ a^t a^t$
Blue-and-buff	Yellow-belly non-agouti dilute	$dd\ aa^t,\ dd\ a^t a^t$
Chocolate-and-buff or Brown-and-tan	Yellow-belly non-agouti brown	$bb\ aa^t,\ bb\ a^t a^t$
Yellow-belly gray	Yellow-belly agouti	$A^{II} A,\ A^{II} a$ or $A\ a^t$
Tricolor	May refer to several combinations, the most common of which is probably yellow-belly non-agouti spotted	$a^t a^t\ ss,\ a^t a\ ss$
Mexican	Recessive hairless	$hr\ hr$
Japanese waltzer	Usually non-agouti piebald waltzer	$aa\ ss\ v$
Short ears	Short ears	$se\ se$

Some of the more common fancy varieties of mice are figured in color by Schuster (*157*) and Little (*110*).

V

NORMAL INHERITANCE

Indeed they (white mice) always bring forth white ones
— Pallas, 1766

For many years it has been known that when white mice are crossed with pure-bred grays, the immediate offspring will be gray and in the second generation albinos will reappear (*36*). The true nature of this transmission, however, was first clearly understood in 1900, when Mendel's Law was rediscovered [1]

Work since that time has shown that the majority of house-mouse characters are inherited in the same simple fashion as albinism. Most of the fancy characters are recessive like albinism, which, when crossed with the wild gray type, produces all grays in the first generation and one recessive out of four in the second generation.

The mechanics of such inheritance is clearly known. The physical determiners underlying these hereditary variations are located in the minute rod-shaped bodies (chromosomes) within the nucleus of each cell of the body. In all mouse body-cells there are twenty kinds of these chromosomes (see Fig. 9) and two of each kind, one of each pair having been received from the father and one from the mother. These chromosomes are reduced from the diploid (double) number to the haploid (single) number at the formation of the gametes (eggs and sperm), so that each gamete contains only one of each pair. When two gametes unite (an egg with

[1] Iltis, 1924 (*80*), p 68, says "We have already heard from Fr Hornish and Inspector Nowotny that Mendel raised mice in one of his two rooms, and not only white ones but also grays, and crossed them with each other. It is very possible that through these more dramatic researches the revelation of dominance and segregation appeared to him for the first time. Indeed, he mentions nothing about it. This is not to be wondered at because industry in natural science at once made an ecclesiast suspicious in the eyes of many clerical zealots to whom the undertaking of animal breeding appeared highly immoral"

a sperm) to form an embryo, the double number is again restored.

A pure-bred gray-coated mouse receives a determiner for pigment development (*C*) from its father and one from its mother. When its gametes are formed, each will contain a single pigment determiner. Hence, in matings with another pure-bred gray, a pair of pigment determiners will enter into each embryo and nothing but pure-bred pigmented young will be produced.

In like fashion an albino receives one determiner for albinism (*c*) from its father and another from its mother, and

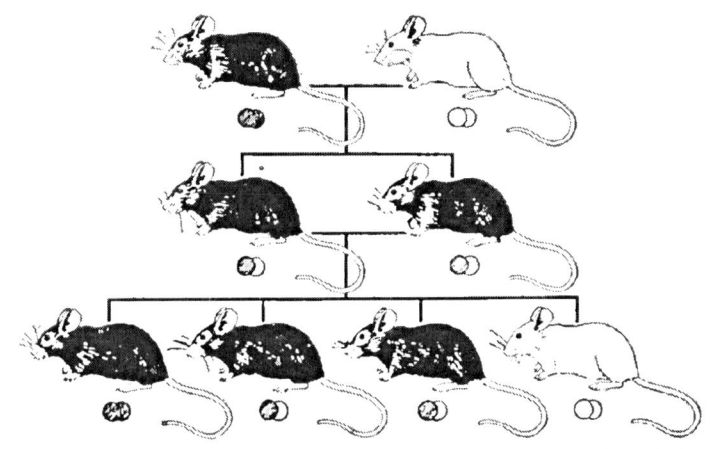

Fig. 6. Diagram illustrating the inheritance of a simple, recessive, mendelizing unit-character such as albinism. Black wafer = *C* gene, white wafer = *c* gene.

produces gametes each bearing a determiner for albinism. Thus, when two albinos are mated together their offspring will receive a determiner for albinism from each parent and hence all are albinos.

If an albino is mated with a pure-bred gray, the albino will contribute an albino determiner (*c*) and the gray will contribute a pigment determiner (*C*) (see Fig. 6). It so happens that the pigment determiner in this case completely dominates over the albino determiner and the cross-bred offspring are pigmented, giving no evidence that they carry an albino determiner. A cross-bred gray carrying albinism produces two kinds of germ cells in equal numbers, half containing the pigment determiner and half containing the albino determiner. Now if two cross-bred grays, each carrying an albino determiner, be mated, the two kinds of germ cells (C and c) will come together purely at random and the offspring will appear in the proportions of 1 pure-bred pigmented 2 cross-bred pigmented 1 pure-bred albino The visible classes will be 3 pigmented (containing C) 1 albino

	Gametes of father		
	C	c	
Gametes C	CC	Cc	Combinations among
of mother c	Cc	cc	the offspring

An actual experiment of this sort (combined data from Little (*110*) and Keeler (*87*)), produced 2994 pigmented young and 1029 albinos or a ratio of 2 91 to 1 the theoretical expectation being 3017 75 pigmented. 1005 75 albinos

Some of the mouse genes have more than two alternative forms or different chemical states The color gene (C) has at least four such allelomorphs in mice. These are (1) normal pigmentation (C), (2) chinchilla (c^{ch}), (3) extreme dilution or Himalayan albinism (c^H), (4) complete albinism (c)

Each member of the series dominates in crosses over those which follow it in the same series. That is, when an animal bears heredity for any two of these characters, the one appearing first in the list will be expressed in the coat. For example, if a chinchilla be crossed with an albino, the first generation will be chinchillas and the second generation will contain an average of 3 chinchillas to 1 albino No more than two members of such a factor series may exist in a single individual (one in each of the two chomosomes making up a particular pair)

If a normally pigmented animal carrying a chinchilla factor be crossed with an extreme-dilute animal carrying albinism, the first generation will consist of equal numbers of normally pigmented animals and of chinchillas Half each of the normals and of the chinchillas will carry extreme dilution and half will carry albinism.

	Gametes C	c^{ch}
Gametes c^H	$C\ c^H$ normally pigmented	$c^{ch}\ c^H$ chinchilla
c	$C\ c$ normally pigmented	$c^{ch}\ c$ chinchilla

Zygotes

If these hybrid-generation animals be mated at random four kinds of germ cells will be formed in equal numbers and will unite also at random, producing on the average 7 normals, 5 chinchillas, 3 extreme dilutes, and 1 albino. Of the 7 normals, 1 will be pure bred, 2 will carry chinchilla, 2 will carry extreme dilution, and 2 will carry albinism. Of the 5 chinchillas, 1 will be pure bred, 2 will carry extreme dilution, and 2 will carry albinism. Of the 3 extreme dilutes, 1 will be pure bred, and 2 will carry albinism. The 1 albino will be pure bred. See diagram.

	Gametes C	c^{ch}	c^H	c
C	CC normal pigment	Cc^{ch} normal pigment	Cc^H normal pigment	Cc normal pigment
c^{ch}	$c^{ch}C$ normal pigment	$c^{ch}c^{ch}$ chinchilla	$c^{ch}c^H$ chinchilla	$c^{ch}c$ chinchilla
Gametes c^H	c^HC normal pigment	c^Hc^{ch} chinchilla	c^Hc^H extreme dilute	c^Hc extreme dilute
c	cC normal pigment	cc^{ch} chinchilla	c^Hc extreme dilute	cc albino

Suppose we have a mouse bearing two independent unit-characteristics (borne in different chromosomes), for example, rodless and albinism. The determiner for the albino character lies in one chromosome pair and that for rodless in an entirely different pair. The genetic formula of this mouse with respect to the two characters named will be *rrcc*, while that for a normal-eyed pigmented mouse will be *RRCC*. The gene for rodless is represented by *r*, the gene for normal eye by *R*, the gene for albinism by *c*, the gene for colored coat by *C*.

If we cross a rodless albino with a normal-eyed pigmented mouse all the immediate offspring will be *Rr Cc*. The gene for normal eye dominates over the gene for rodless and thus the offspring are normal eyed. The pigment-forming gene dominates over the albino gene and thus the offspring are pigmented. Yet they carry (recessive) heredity for both rodless and albinism.

These normal-appearing offspring, carrying as recessive genes albinism and rodless, form four kinds of gametes in equal numbers, *RC*, *Rc*, *rC*, and *rc*. If two such double heterozygotes be mated together they will produce offspring in the proportion of 9 normal-eyed pigmented, 3 normal-eyed albinos, 3 rodless pigmented, and 1 rodless albino. The checkerboard below shows how these combinations could arise through the random union (*48*) of these four types of gametes.

	Gametes			
	RC	*Rc*	*rC*	*rc*
RC	*RC* *RC*	*Rc* *RC*	*rC* *RC*	*rc* *RC*
Rc	*RC* *Rc*	*Rc* *Rc*	*rC* *Rc*	*rc* *Rc*
rC	*RC* *rC*	*Rc* *rC*	*rC* *rC*	*rc* *rC*
rc	*RC* *rc*	*Rc* *rc*	*rC* *rc*	*rc* *rc*

Gametes — Zygotes

An experiment (*87*) of this kind yielded 165 normal-eyed pigmented, 64 normal-eyed albinos, 51 rodless pigmented, and 29 rodless albinos, or a ratio of 8.5 : 3.3 : 2.6 : 1.5

	Normal-eyed pigmented	Normal-eyed albinos	Rodless pigmented	Rodless albinos
Found	165	64	51	29
Expected	173.7	57.9	57.9	19.3

If the double heterozygotes be mated back to the parent pure for the two recessive characteristics, four classes of offspring will be expected in equal numbers, namely, normal-eyed pigmented, normal-eyed albino, rodless pigmented rodless albino. This test (87) yielded of those classes respectively 66 : 54 : 68 : 51 or ratios of 1.1 : .99 : 1.1 : .93.

Gametes of double heterozygotes

		RC	Rc	rC	rc
		RC rc Normal-eyed pigmented	Rc rc Normal-eyed pigmented	rC rc Rodless pigmented	rc rc Rodless albino
Gametes of double recessive	rc				
Found		66	54	68	51
Expected		59.7	59.7	59.7	59.7

The gene for two or more unit characters may lie at different points or "loci" upon the same chromosome, a relationship known as linkage. Linkage is measured by the amount of crossing-over, or recombination. Ordinarily in the formation of gametes the two chromosomes of an homologous pair, which have lain side by side in immature germ cells, separate at maturation and one passes to each daughter cell. Each functional gamete (egg or sperm) thus contains one representative (not two) of each gene. The chances are even that it will be the representative derived from the father or that derived from the mother.

Occasionally chromosomes break (see Fig 7) transversely while lying elongated in pairs previous to the reduction division. When the break is repaired the broken ends may become united differently from before. The chromosomes which originally bore RC and rc respectively may after a

NORMAL INHERITANCE 41

"crossing-over", bear *Rc* and *rC*. The percentage of cases (times in a hundred) in which crossing-over occurs is called the crossover percentage. The nearer together two genes lie in the same chromosome, the fewer chances there are for breaks to occur between them resulting in recombination or crossing-over. Hence the percentage of crossing-over is taken as a measure of the nearness together of genes or of the linkage strength (16) between them.

In cases where linkage is involved, new combinations (recombinations) of two characters may be difficult to obtain.

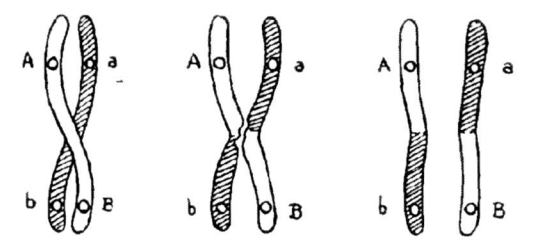

Fig. 7. Diagram of a pair of chromosomes showing the linkage relationship of two pairs of genes before, during, and after a crossing-over.

Suppose we select a mouse bearing two genes located in the same chromosome, for example rodless and silver (*rrss*). Should we cross this rodless-silver to a normal-eyed unsilvered mouse (*RSRS*) the offspring will be *rsRS* and will be normal-eyed unsilvered. When these animals form gametes, *r* and *s* being in the same physical chromosome will behave ordinarily as units as also will *R* and *S* for a like reason. Hence there will be ordinarily two, and only two, kinds of gametes, namely, *rs* and *RS*. If two such animals are mated together they will produce ordinarily but two types of offspring: normal-eyed unsilvered (*RSRS* or *RSrs*) and rodless silver (*rsrs*). But when there is a crossover, two other types of gametes are produced (*rS* and *Rs*), making possible the occurrence of occasional rodless unsilvered animals (*rSrS* or *rsrS*) and normal-eyed silvers (*RsRs* and *rsRs*). We may detect the percentage of crossovers between *r* and *s* by crossing an *rsRS* animal to an *rsrs* (see Fig. 8).

	Gametes of *rsRS* parent			
Gametes of *rrss* parent		*RS*	*Rs*	*rS*	*rs*
	rs	*RS* *rs* Normal-eyed unsilvered	*Rs* *rs* Normal-eyed silver	*rS* *rs* Rodless unsilvered	*rs* *rs* Rodless silver

Crossover classes

If the characters silver and rodless were not linked, we should expect equal numbers of all four classes. If they are linked, we expect the second and third classes to be small in comparison with the first and fourth. The second and third

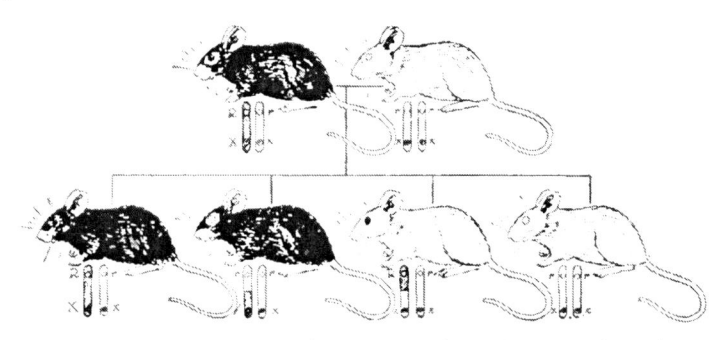

Fig. 8. Diagram of a back-cross illustrating the linkage between rodless retina (r) and silver pelage (s). Animals with unshaded eyes are rodless.

classes are produced only from gametes in the genesis of which a crossover has occurred between silver and rodless. A back-cross of the kind described (98) gave 9 unsilvered normals, 1 unsilvered rodless, 1 silver normal, and 5 silver rodless. More extensive breeding tests indicate that a crossover takes place between silver and rodless at the formation of about 12 per cent of the gametes.

If three determiners are located at different points in the same chromosome, as are albinism (172), shaker (126), and pink-eye dilution (172), we may determine their relative positions by the percentage of crossovers obtained in breeding experiments. If a crossover occurs between albinism and shaker 3 times out of a hundred and between shaker and pink-eye dilution 15 times out of a hundred and between albinism and pink-eye dilution 18 times out of a hundred, then the three genes must lie in the order albino, shaker, and pink-eye dilution The indicated distance between albino and shaker is about one-sixth that between albino and pink-eye dilution.

In Fig 9 a number of determiners (genes) for mouse unit-characters are represented as located upon diagrammatic chromosomes of the mouse, to illustrate the genetic

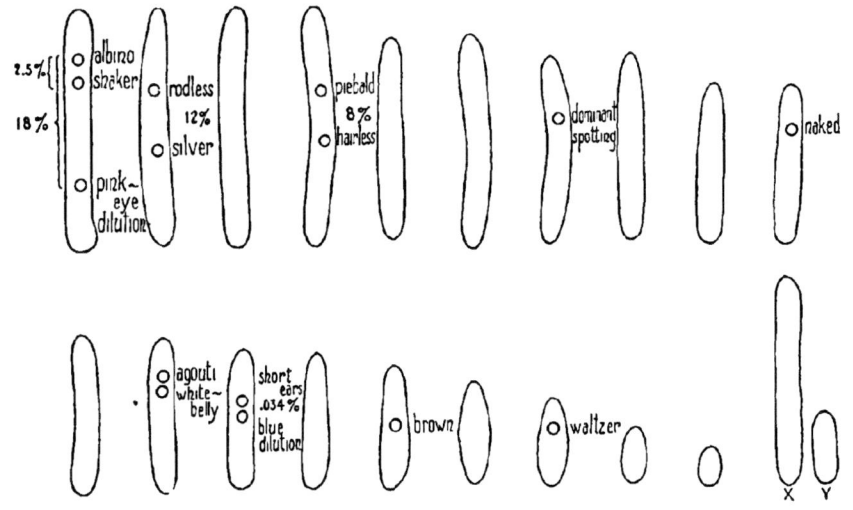

Fig 9 Diagram of chromosomes of the house mouse (22) with genes for unit characters distributed arbitrarily among them to show genetic independence or linkage of the characters

independence or linkage found experimentally to exist between these determiners

Besides the two linkage systems already mentioned (*172*), linkage has been shown to exist between recessive spotting and recessive hairless (*161*), and between short ears and dilution (*64, 159*) It is possible, as already suggested, that agouti and white-belly may also be linked characters, rather than allelomorphs

According to present data, known hereditary characters have their determining genes located in 9 of the 20 pairs of chromosomes of the house mouse. It is reasonable to suppose that some day characters will be found in the remaining 11 pairs as well as other genes within those chromosomes already bearing determiners for fancy variations

VI

ABNORMAL INHERITANCE

THE characters non-agouti, pink-eye dilution, blue dilution, brown, recessive spotting, waltzer, rodless, shaker, and the albino series of allelomorphs seem to be recessive unit-characters and to behave according to the rule for simple Mendelian inheritance. Varieties characterized by these all breed true because they are homozygous. Yellow-belly behaves as a dominant unit-character and breeds true only when homozygous. Yellow and dominant spotting do not breed true but produce only 50 per cent of offspring possessing the characters in question, because they are dominant lethals and so cannot be made homozygous.

Normal Overlaps. Silver behaves as a recessive unit-character but seemingly does not always breed true because some silvered animals are with difficulty recognized as such. Silvered mice throw a certain percentage of animals of such a low grade of silver that they may not be distinguished readily from non-silvered animals, although they are genetically silvers. Such animals which are genetically of a mutant type but somatically are capable of classification as of the normal type are known as normal overlaps.

Dominant Lethals. Two of the unit-characters of mice, namely yellow and dominant spotting, are dominant lethals. By this we mean that animals bearing one factor for the character exhibit the character, but that animals bearing two factors for the character are non-viable. Thus, all yellow mice carry a non-yellow factor as a recessive. When two yellows are mated together they produce on the average one homozygous yellow which dies, two yellows heterozygous like themselves, and one non-yellow animal, as was first pointed out by Cuénot (*24*).

The same is true for dominant spotting. Two dominant-spotted animals produce on an average one homozygous

ABNORMAL INHERITANCE

dominant-spotted animal which dies of anaemia (*115*), two dominant spotted (heterozygotes), and one non-dominant-spotted animal. Strains of dominant spotting exist which throw self animals as recessives. (See Fig. 21.) These are the non-dominant-spotted class. Other strains, known as black-eyed whites, are homozygous for recessive spotting and consequently produce piebald animals instead of selfs, as the non-dominant-spotted class.

Hereditary Sterility. Dominant hairless (naked) individuals which are heterozygous are often produced, but are usually sterile. In one case a homozygous naked female produced young but had no milk to nurse them. Possibly the mutation which affected the hair follicles also disturbed the

	Gametes N	n
Gametes N	NN Homozygous naked (sterile)	Nn Heterozygous naked
n	Nn Heterozygous naked	nn Normal

processes of mammary development or secretion. Dominant hairless stocks are maintained by mating heterozygous individuals with each other or by mating heterozygotes to normals. In both types of cross one half the progeny are wasters, that is, are not of the desired type, heterozygous naked.

	Gametes n	n
Gametes N	Nn Heterozygous naked	Nn Heterozygous naked
n	nn Normal	nn Normal

Recessive hairless usually produces sterile females and fertile males and hence the strain is readily preserved by mating hairless males to heterozygous females The resulting hairless males are crossed to their heterozygous sisters, and so on

A certain amount of sterility is encountered in short-eared mice This may or may not be associated in some fashion with the short-ear character but is complicated in its inheritance

The sterility often found among waltzers is usually due to the fact that these animals are very delicate and require the best of care in a very special environment Under ideal conditions they breed well. They are, however, poor mothers and their young should when possible be given to a foster mother of some non-waltzing variety to nurse.

VII

THE BREEDING OF MICE IN LABORATORIES

Mating Habits The œstrous cycle (*2*) of the mouse lasts from three to four days In only a few hours within this cycle will the female permit the amours of a male, at other times she avoids his attentions by slipping quietly into the nest or by climbing up the side of the cage.

During the receptive period her reactions to courtship change completely When her suitor approaches, she often rears upon her haunches, throws her paws up in a defensive attitude, closes her eyes, and gives a characteristic short squeak The male nervously licks her face, sniffs at her genitals, and attempts to mount The female often runs away into the nest or up the side of her cage only to return to the former trysting place There are numerous unsuccessful attempts at copulation before the completed act takes place

The secretions of the male form a soft vaginal plug which quickly hardens, cementing the vagina shut and thus preventing escape of the sperm until after fertilization (*125*) of the eggs is accomplished The vaginal plug is usually lost within twenty-four hours

Uterine Development (*129, 81*). The sperm ascend the genital tracts within a few hours after copulation and fertilize the eggs as they are shed from the follicles before they enter the uterus. The fertilized eggs descend into the uterus where they implant about the fifth day. At this time development has progressed to about the primitive streak stage About the eighth day, at a stage corresponding to that of the three-day chick, all the fœtal organs are laid down. The cerebral ganglia are growing out, and the limb buds are forming, while the heart has long been pumping blood through the fœtal arches The retina has invaginated and the lens is formed.

The young are born usually between the nineteenth and twenty-first days after mating (*103, 29*). In Japan wild house mice and those of the fancy are often termed "twenty-one-day mice" on account of the length of the gestation period

Birth Just prior to parturition the female may be observed to become restless. During this period she may construct an elaborate nest by winding strands of nesting tissue to form a ball, tucking in loose ends here and there.

At the birth of young, the reactions of the mother seem to vary greatly with such factors as her natural temperament, health, company, and the degree of seclusion provided by her cage. Some mice retire to the nest for parturition while others continue their routine reactions about the cage

Reaction to the new-born young may vary from almost completely ignoring them where they happen to drop outside the nest, to birth within the nest followed by careful washing and cuddling.

Four or five minutes of uterine contraction may be required to give birth to a mouseling, followed within a minute by the expulsion of the placenta and perhaps portions of the foetal membranes. The female chews and occasionally devours the placenta.

The new-born mouse is a naked little creature about two and a half centimeters long with well proportioned head, body, and feet. It is unpigmented save for the dark ring of the iris, which is visible through the translucent eyelids The ears are folded forward and sealed

The new-born mouse left to itself may remain motionless for as long as a minute before it gives its first tiny gasp, followed by another and another These gasps are continued at irregular intervals, often accompanied by violent contractions of the body and especially the breathing muscles. Within five minutes the mouseling is breathing regularly and lying quietly except perhaps for an occasional twitch of a leg or a sucking movement of the mouth.

Nursing takes place as soon as the mother huddles over

the young mouse subsequent to its metamorphosis into an air-breathing creature, at times perhaps even before it is dry. The first period of nursing may continue as long as fifteen hours, if the mother is not interrupted

Under poor conditions some mice will not nurse their young In case a mouse refuses to nurse young of great value to the investigator, they should be fostered If young mice have nursed it is evident, because milk contained in the stomach shows through the left side as a cream-colored crescent.

Growth. As with most helpless infants, during the first period of their lives, the reactions of young mice are confined chiefly to nursing and sleeping, while their bodies grow rapidly in size and differentiation progresses in the more retarded organs such as those of special sense The rods of the retina, for example, are developed after the fifth day

The pigmented hair within the skin is faintly visible upon the second or third day and is well developed by the eighth day, when the skin becomes scaly, probably due to a shedding of the external surface as dandruff By this time the little mice move blindly about the nest and even venture into the world outside, only to be hustled back in the mouth of their mother, who continually washes, feeds, and looks after them

By the thirteenth day the truancy of these little balls of fur, still unsteady upon their feet, becomes too great for their attentive mother, who still repeatedly carries them back to the nest They occasionally escape to a sequestered corner of the cage, where they test things with their paws, noses, tongues, and vibrissæ They sit and wash their faces, nibble morsels of food, and blink at the light with their newly opened eyes.

In the childhood of the mouse there has been observed no period of play such as young rats enjoy when they mouth, kick, tussle, clutch, and roll with each other However, between the fifteenth and twenty-fifth days young mice unused to handling are more restless and more active than usual, squeaking, scampering, leaping, and seeking to hide themselves at the slightest noise or motion. The degree of this activity also has a genetic basis, because members of certain strains are much more active than members of other strains.

By the thirteenth day the young mouse is almost an adult save in size and sex differentiation. Sex maturity is usually reached between the second and third months, although mice increase a small amount in size during the several succeeding months.

Fostering. Fostering is often desirable where the female is of a feeble strain, is a poor mother, or is one from which a maximum number of offspring is desired.

In fostering it is a good practice to employ as nurses females which are first-generation offspring of a cross between two inbred varieties which show great vigor, although any docile vigorous female will do. A number of these prospective nurse mothers are mated simultaneously with those whose young are to be fostered so that nurses will be available when the desirable young are born.

Some foster mothers object to an exchange of young, especially if the mice to be fostered are younger than her own litter. The foster litter and the foster mother's own litter are shaken together gently by some investigators in order that the foster mice may obtain the odor of the foster mother's nest and be more acceptable. The mice to be fostered are picked out and given to the foster mother, while the foster mother's own litter are killed.

If a female mouse has not nursed much, she will usually breed within twenty-four hours after parturition.

Killing. Some investigators prefer to drop all discard mice into a covered jar containing a piece of cotton saturated with ether, although simple mechanical methods of terminating their existence are both adequate and painless.

Parasites. Even with the best of care a mouse colony may occasionally be infested with fleas, mites, or lice to the extent that they prevent breeding, although these parasites seldom prove fatal. Pyrethrum powder or pulverized tobacco dusted upon the animals from time to time are good preventive measures. However, should the infestation persist, the mice may be individually caught by the tail, dipped in a warm, very dilute solution of stock-dip, and allowed to dry in a warm place. If metal cages are employed, the nest and food may be removed and the whole cage dipped, mice and all. We have found Parke Davis and Company's Kreso-Dip satisfactory for this purpose.

Mice are occasionally attacked by a white fungus which grows upon their ears. It is difficult to eradicate and hence if the affected animal may be spared it should be killed. If the fungus affects only the tip of an ear when discovered, it may frequently be eliminated by clipping off the ear below the affected region. Adult mouse ears seldom bleed when snipped off, but if they should, a little sodium subsulphate powder will quickly stop the flow.

Mice sometimes harbor a tapeworm for which the cat serves as definitive host. Accordingly, it is advisable to exclude all cats from the mouse room. There are other more obvious reasons why cats are undesirable tenants of a murarium.

Diseases. Some strains of fancy mice are affected with hereditary tumors. Those involving the mammæ of the female are the most common. If a tumorous female is very valuable, occasionally a single litter of mice may be procured from her after surgical removal of the growth. As a general practice animals bearing tumors should be discarded as the results seldom justify the efforts to save them.

Mice are susceptible to a number of non-specific organism-borne diseases (*171, 133*), such as surra (*Trypanosoma evansi*), apoplectic septicemia, fakosis (*Micrococcus caprinus*), fowl cholera (*Bacterium choleræ gallinarum*), trichosis (*Trichinella spiralis*), the disease caused by *Bacillus piliformis*, sarcosporidiosis, botryomycosis, and coccidiosis. These diseases will seldom be encountered in a well-kept mouse colony, and hence a mere mention of them will suffice here.

By far the worst disease among laboratory mice is paratyphoid (*175*) (often known as diarrhœa) caused by *Bacillus typhi murium.* If one can possibly spare the mice, it is advisable to kill off each day all sick animals and sterilize the cages at once. Some adult mice are not killed outright by the disease, but they remain carriers of the condition and may do much damage by spreading it. This disease is usually fatal to animals between fifteen and twenty-five days of age. A few recover, and if these are females they may be normal and reproduce, but if they are males they will usually be sterile, due to the fact that the poisonous, diarrhœic feces "scald" the scrotal region, causing the formation of scar tissue. The stiff scar tissue prevents the descent of the testicles necessary for fertility. Thus it is advisable in every case to kill all young affected males. If valuable young females are preserved, they should not be kept in the mouse room.

By the enumeration of the above pathological conditions and insistence upon drastic measures to eliminate disease from the mouse colony, it is not intended to give the impression that mice are weak and susceptible to all sorts of sickness, making them difficult to raise in quantity. There is no limit to the number of healthy mice which may be maintained in a well-tended murarium. Five thousand is not an unusual size of colony for an experimental laboratory.

Breeding Cages. There are a number of practicable designs for successful breeding cages, but the most satisfactory are those which provide adequately for certain requirements peculiar to the mouse. The design of the cage should take into consideration size convenient for handling, space occupied, dry feed, closed water bottles, changeable nesting material, absorption of urine, and ease of sterilization. A mouse cage meeting these requirements has been developed at the Bussey Institution (see Fig. 10).

The cage is made of galvanized-iron wire netting of $\frac{1}{3}$ inch mesh. The dimensions of the cage are 12 inches long, 7 inches wide, and 7 inches high. It rests upon half an inch of sawdust in a galvanized-iron pan 15 inches long, $13\frac{1}{2}$ inches wide, and $3\frac{1}{2}$ inches deep. Two cages nest side by side in each pan. These pans with the contained cages are kept upon racks of dimensions to accommodate them.

The cage proper has a sloping front provided with a galvanized-iron door which is held shut by gravity and the weight of the water bottle. The iron door is convenient as a memorandum space for numbers or notes not recorded in the official register.

A dog biscuit is wired to the rear wall. The cage is provided with a handful of shredded tissue paper for nest ma-

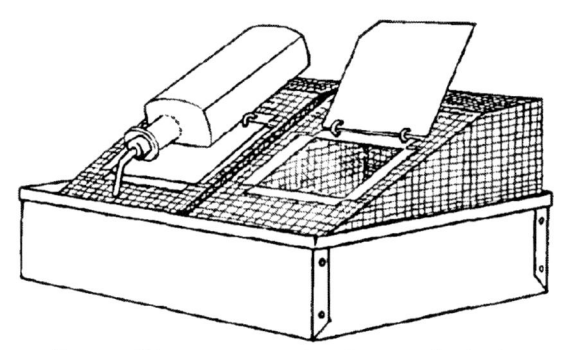

FIG. 10. Wire mouse cage used at the Bussey Institution.

terial and with a feed dish. A numbered metal tag for cage identification is wired to the sloping front, or the number may be painted on the iron door.

Once a week the cages should be cleaned with a stiff brush, provided with fresh nesting tissue, fresh sawdust, and clean food dishes, and about once a month they should be washed.

Sanitary Precautions. Because mice are subject to several infectious diseases, cages should be of a material which may be readily sterilized. If cages are made of metal they may be sterilized by immersion in boiling soapy water, brushing, and then dipping in a solution of "Kreso" or other disinfectant. Cages should be disinfected at least once a month in absence of disease and oftener if the colony is infected. Cages in which diseased animals have lived should be disinfected immediately.

Animals dying from no matter what cause should be removed from cages at once, because the carcasses are often partially eaten by other mice and disease may thus be spread.

Water Water standing in an open dish in a mouse cage becomes quickly contaminated with urine and feces and is unfit for drinking. The greatest difficulty, however, is that active mice will continually run through any open water dish, very frequently splashing water upon their fur. Often they become chilled and contract pneumonia, which usually proves fatal.[1]

For these reasons a closed drinking-water supply is best. A bottle fitted with a rubber cork pierced by a glass tube is most satisfactory. The glass tubing should be drawn to a nipple and the end smoothed in the flame, because water will drip through a large opening. This provides constantly a hanging drop which is licked by the mice when they desire it.

Records Every animal should be numbered and registered with regard to individual number, sex, description, known recessive characters, parents, date of birth, and often disposition and date.

A card index should be kept, bearing the numbers of the cages upon the guide cards and a card filled out for each animal with data on individual number, sex, purpose and date of mating, and cage number. This should be filed at the proper place within the index.

When a female becomes pregnant, she should be given a separate cage, because, with other mice in the cage, some mothers become excited and kill their young. New-born mice are often killed by males or more often still by other females in the cage. Date of birth, record number of the father, and information concerning the young not yet registered may be jotted down upon the card of the mother.

Numbering A satisfactory system of marking mice for identification purposes is to punch the ears with a chick punch. The following simple system of position marks is used almost exclusively by American geneticists. The first

---

[1] The practice of providing open water dishes may have occasioned the statement of Aristotle concerning the white mice of Pontus that if they drink water they will die.

three numerals, 1, 2, and 3, are denoted by holes in the ear at top, side, and bottom respectively. The second three, 4, 5, and 6, are represented by notches in the edge of the ear at top, side, and bottom. The next three numerals, 7, 8, and 9, are indicated by combinations of two notches, 7 being notches at both top and side, 8 being notches at both side and bottom, and 9 being notches at both top and bottom.

With this system, employing the right ear for units and the left ear for tens, one may number animals from 1 to 99. One hundred has a hole in the center of each ear, but may be distinguished from 200, 300, 700 etc., by age, color, parents, cage number, and other records. By these data one may also identify mice whose individual record numbers bear the same last two digits.

Temperature. Mice are quite sensitive to changes in temperature. A cold draft from a window may prove fatal to a high percentage of a colony within a single night. Even the opening and shutting of outside doors on cold winter days may chill the mice considerably. The optimum condition is a room regulated between 70° and 80° F. both day and night. Animals suffering slightly from exposure may wheeze chronically, but appear in fair health and even breed. This condition is known to the fanciers as "singing" or "asthma."

Food. Food should be readily available to mice at all times. A mouse that spends more than twenty-four hours at one time without food is in grave danger of starving to death. If only a meager amount of food is present, life may be sustained, but the animals will not reproduce. A suitable ration for mice measured by weight consists of

240 parts rolled oats
30 parts powdered skim milk
8 parts cod-liver oil
1 part salt

A formula for rat feed, which is probably satisfactory also for mice, has been recently prepared by Maynard (*131*) consisting in parts by weight as follows:

Linseed-oil meal	15
Ground malted barley	10
Wheat red-dog flour	22
Dried skim milk	15
Oat flour	15
Yellow corn meal	20
Steam bone meal	1
Ground limestone	1
Salt	1
Total	100

As mice are so dependent for health upon the constant availability of food, it is advisable to have present in their cages at all times a balanced-ration dog biscuit upon which they may gnaw if other food has been consumed between feeding hours

For mice to breed well, greens are desirable in the form of lettuce or clover once or twice a week. Caution must be observed in the feeding of lettuce that all tainted or rotten spots be removed, for mice will eat these along with the good portions and may be made sick by so doing. Hemp seed is advised from time to time. According to fanciers, animals suffering from lack of greens may become scurvied, but this condition disappears when they are properly fed.

A Closed Feeding Can. Mice delight in digging in an open dish full of food. They waste great quantities of food by kicking it out of the dish, and contaminate with their feces that remaining in the dish. In order to eliminate these two undesirable features of the open feeding dish a closed feeding can has been recently devised and is in use at the Bussey Institution (see Fig. 11). This consists of a half-pound coffee can approximately 4 inches high and $3\frac{1}{2}$ inches in diameter. In the side of the can is cut a 1-inch square hole, the lower edge of which is $\frac{1}{2}$ inch from the bottom of the can. The top and sides of the hole are faced with a strip of tin projecting $\frac{1}{2}$ inch into the can, to prevent the fall of food near the entrance. A wedge-shaped cage made of galvanized-wire cloth of $\frac{1}{3}$ inch mesh is soldered in place with the large open end of the wedge over the entrance and projecting about

2½ inches into the can. The edge of the wedge rests upon the floor of the can and its sides extend outward on either side of the opening from which they are about ½ inch distant laterally at the opening.

The cage is small enough so the hind quarters of the adult mouse must remain outside the can while its hind feet rest on the edge of the entrance. These features prevent both fecal

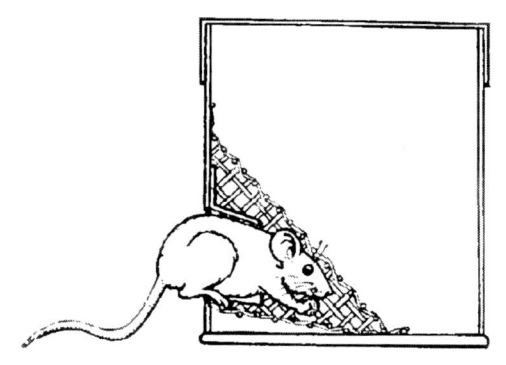

FIG. 11. Sectional view of feeding can.

contamination and the kicking of food out of the can. The mesh of the screen-wire wedge is fine enough to prevent dry ration containing rolled oats from sifting into the feeding chamber. The mouse simply reaches through the mesh and pulls down what food he desires, eats it in place, and backs out of the feeder when satisfied. If it is desired to give the Maynard ration in the closed feeder, it should be mixed in equal parts with rolled oats, because the Maynard ration is finely ground and sifts through the screen wire.

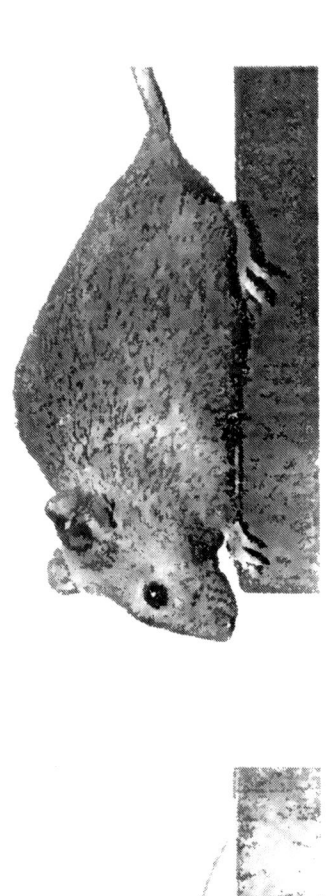

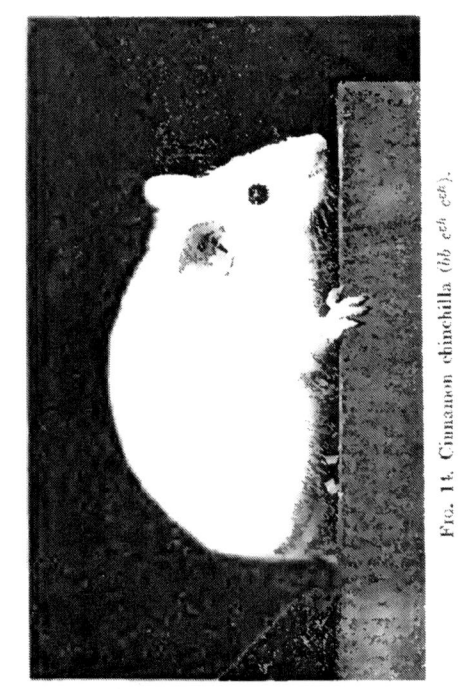

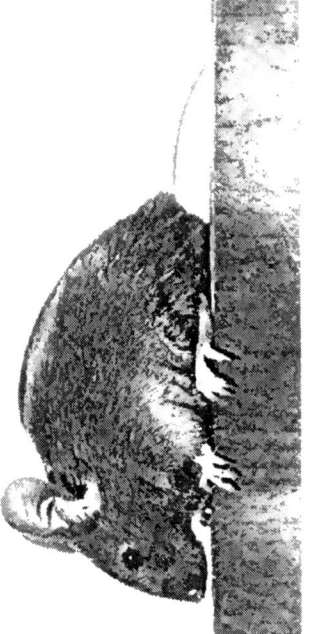

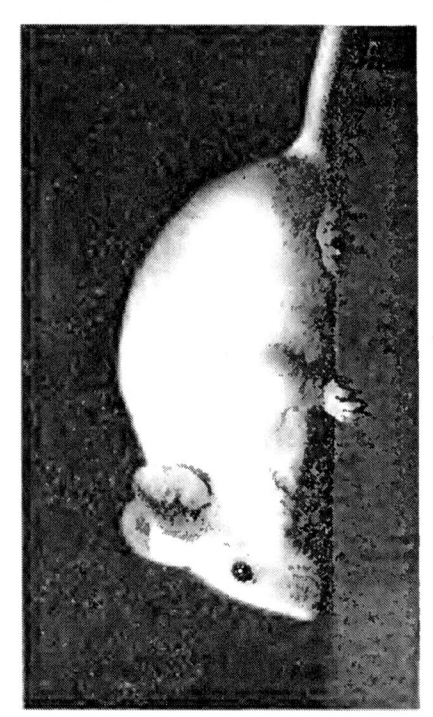

Fig. 12. Gray (wild coated).
Fig. 13. Brown extreme dilute ($bb\ e^d\ e^d$).
Fig. 14. Cinnamon chinchilla ($bb\ e^{ch}\ e^{ch}$).
Fig. 15. Albino (cc).

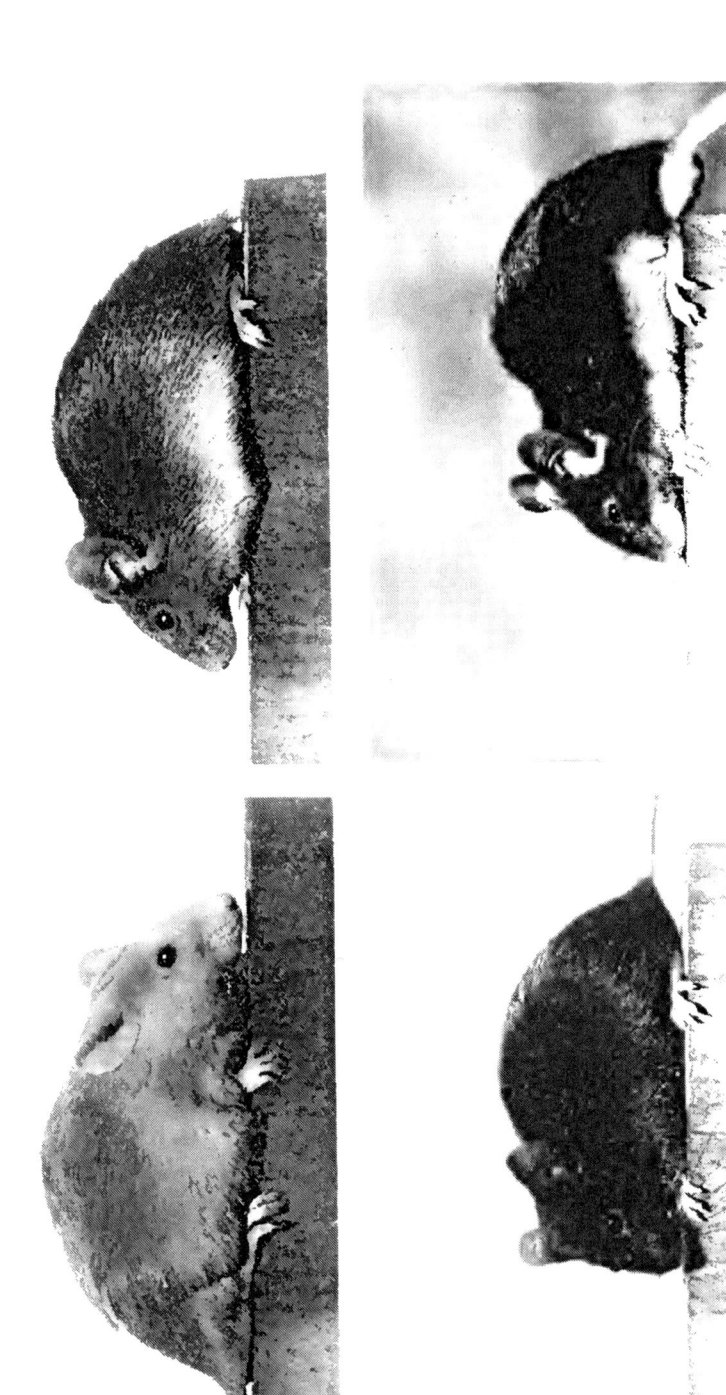

Fig. 18. Sooty yellow (A^y a).
Fig. 19. Black-and-tan or white-bellied non-agouti black (a^t a^t).

Fig. 16. Lethal yellow (A^y A^y).
Fig. 17. Non-agouti black (aa).

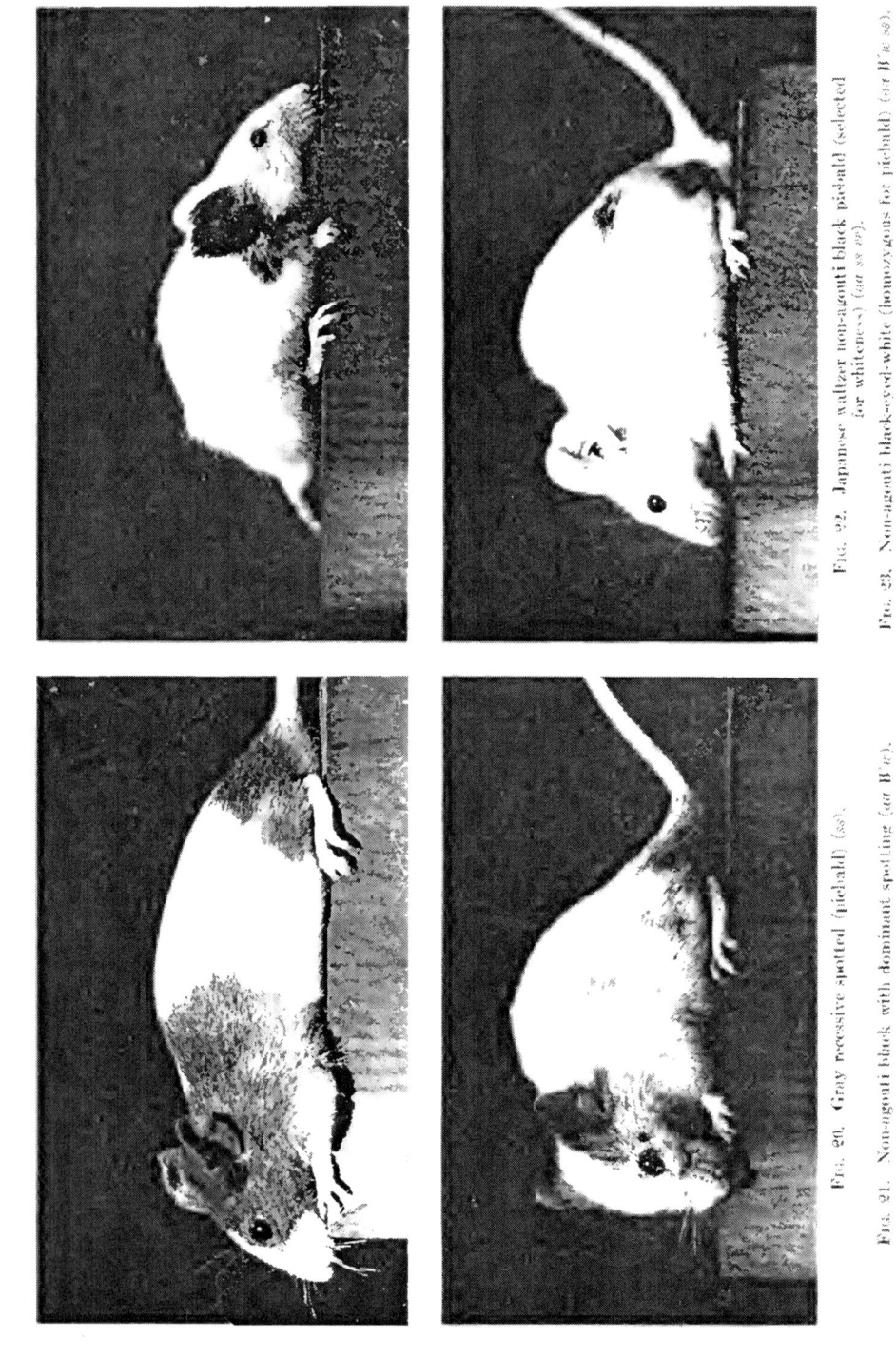

Fig. 20. Gray recessive spotted (piebald) (ss).

Fig. 21. Non-agouti black with dominant spotting (aa W/+).

Fig. 22. Japanese waltzer non-agouti black piebald (selected for whiteness) (aa ss v).

Fig. 23. Non-agouti black-eyed-white (homozygous for piebald) (aa B' a ss).

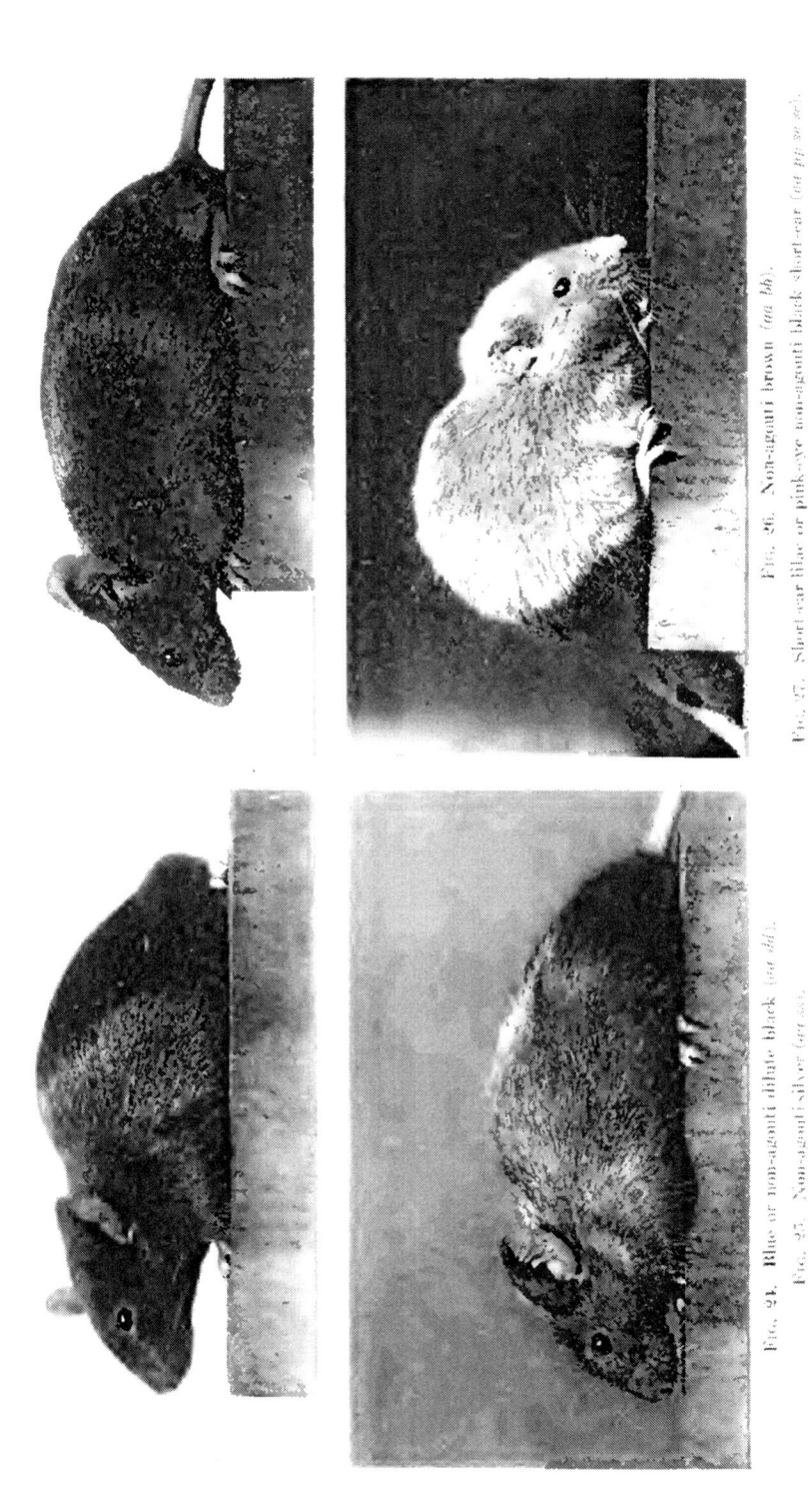

Fig. 24. Blue or non-agouti dilute black (*aa dd*).
Fig. 25. Non-agouti silver (*aa ss*).
Fig. 26. Non-agouti brown (*aa bb*).
Fig. 27. Short-ear blue or pink-eye non-agouti black short-ear (*aa pp se*).

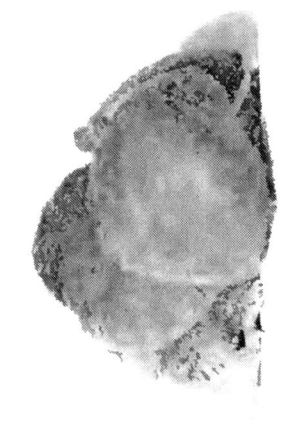

Fig. 28. Heterozygous naked ("naked") (Nn).
Fig. 29. Recessive hairless (hr hr).
Fig. 30. Homozygous naked (NN).
Fig. 31. Non-agouti dilute brown (aa bb dd) having developed two large transplanted tumors.

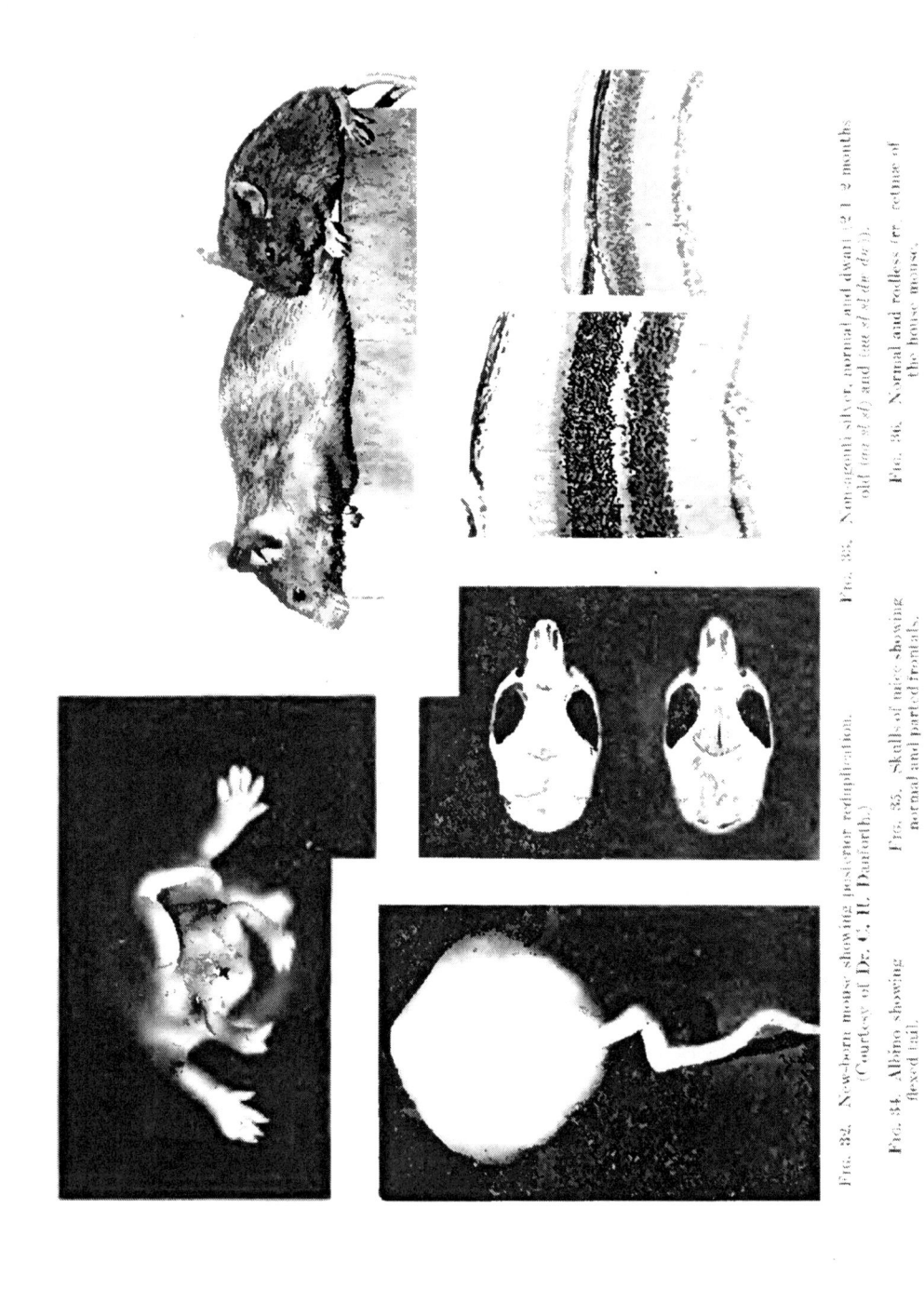

Fig. 32. Newborn mouse showing posterior reduplication. (Courtesy of Dr. C. H. Danforth.)

Fig. 33. Non-agouti silver, normal and dwarf (2 1-2 months old (wt. 8.8) and one of 81 (wt. 4.9)).

Fig. 34. Albino showing flexed tail.

Fig. 35. Skulls of mice showing normal and parted frontals.

Fig. 36. Normal and earless (or reduce of the house mouse.

(69)

BIBLIOGRAPHY

BIBLIOGRAPHY

1 AELIANUS (c A.D 100), 1774 *Zoo Idiothtos* Book XII, Chap V. Basilæ, Joh Jacobum Flick

2 ALLEN, E , 1922 "The œstrous cycle in the mouse" *Amer Jour. Anat*, Vol 30, pp 297-371

3 ALLEN, G. M , 1904 "The heredity of coat color in mice" *Proc Amer. Acad Arts and Sci*, Vol 40, pp. 61-163

4 ———, 1927 "Murid rodents from the Asiatic expeditions." *Amer Mus Novitates*, No. 270, pp 1-12

5 ARISTOTLE *De Animalibus Historia*, Vol. X

6 BAGG, H J , 1921 'The absence of one kidney associated with hereditary abnormalities in the descendants of X-rayed mice." *Proc Soc Exp Biol and Med*, Vol 21, pp 146-149

7 BARTHOLOMEW, J G 1911 *Atlas of Zoogeography* Edinburgh, John Bartholomew & Co

8 BATESON, W , 1894 *Materials for the Study of Heredity* London

9 ———, 1903 "The present state of knowledge of colour heredity in mice and rats" *Proc Zool Soc* London, Vol 1903, pp 71-99

10 ——— and E R SAUNDERS, 1902 "Experimental studies in the physiology of heredity" *Rept Evol Com Roy Soc*, Pt 1, pp 1-160

11. BLANK, E , 1916 "Die Knickschwanze der Mauser" *Arch Entw. Mech*, Vol 42, pp 333-406

12 BROOKE, H. C , 1926 'Hairless mice" *Jour Hered*, Vol 17, pp 173-174

13. CAMMIDGE, P J and HOWARD, H A H , 1926 "Hyperglycæmia as a Mendelian recessive character in mice" *Jour of Gen*, Vol 16, p 387

14 CAMPBELL, A , 1907 "Mus musculus var Nudo-plicatus" *Zoologist*, 4th Series, Vol 11, pp 1-3

15 CASTLE, W E 1906 "Yellow mice and gametic purity" *Science*, Vol 24, pp 275-281

16 ———, 1916. "Tables of linkage intensities" *Amer Nat*, Vol 50, pp 575-576.

17 ———, 1919 "Studies of heredity in rabbits, rats, and mice." *Carnegie Inst Wash Pub*, No 288

18 CASTLE, W E and ALLEN, G M , 1903. "The heredity of albinism" *Proc Amer Acad Arts and Sci*, Vol 38, pp 603-622

19 ——— and LITTLE, C C , 1909 "Peculiar inheritance of pink eyes among colored mice" *Science*, Vol 30, pp 313-314

20 ——— and LITTLE, C C , 1910 "On a modified Mendelian ratio among yellow mice" *Science*, Vol 32, pp 868-870

21 ——— and WACHTER, W L , 1924 "Variations of linkage in rats and mice *Gen*, Vol 9, pp 1-12

22. Cox, E. K , 1926 "The chromosomes of the mouse " *Jour Morph*, Vol 43, pp 1-14
23. Cuénot, L , 1903-1907 "L'hérédité de la pigmentation chez les souris " *Archv. Zool. Exp. et Gen., N et R.*, Vol. 4, Nos 1, 2, 3, 4, 6, Vol 5, No 1
24. ——, 1908 "Sur quelques anomalies apparentes des proportions mendeliennes " *Archv Zool Exp et Gen*, Vol 4, No 9
25. ——, 1911 "L'hérédité chez les souris " *Fest zum Andenken Gregor Mendel*, pp 214-222
26. ——, 1928 Génétique des souris *Biblio Gen*, Vol 4
27. Danforth, C H , 1930 "Developmental anomalies in a special strain of mice " *Amer Jour Anat*, Vol 45, pp 275-287
28. —— and De Aberle, S B , 1927 "Functional interrelation of certain genes in the development of the mouse." *Gen*, Vol. 12, pp 340-347
29. Daniel, J. F , 1910 "Observations on the gestation period of white mice " *Jour Exp Zool*, Vol 9, pp 865-877
30. ——, 1912 "Mice, their breeding and rearing for scientific purposes " *Amer Nat*, Vol 46, pp 591-604
31. Darbishire, A D , 1902 "First report on the results of crossing Japanese waltzing mice with European albino races ' *Biometrika*, Vol 2, pp 101-104
32. ——, 1904 "On the result of crossing Japanese waltzing mice with albino mice " *Biometrika*, Vol. 3, pp. 1-51.
33. Davenport, C B , 1900 "Review of von Guaita's experiments in breeding mice ' *Biol Bull* Vol 2, pp 121-128
34. ——, 1904. "Color inheritance in mice " *Science*, Vol 19, pp 110-114
35. Davies, C J , 1912 *Fancy Mice* 5th Edition London, L Upcott Gill
36. Darwin, C , 1868 *The Variation of Animals and Plants under Domestication* London, John Murray.
37. De Aberle, S F , 1925 "Hereditary anemia in mice, and its relation to dominant spotting." *Amer Nat*, Vol 59, pp 327-335
38. Detlefsen, J A , 1916 "Pink-eyed white mice carrying the color factor " *Amer Nat*, Vol 50, pp 46-49
39. ——, 1921 "A new mutation in the house mouse " *Amer Nat*, Vol 55, pp. 469-473.
40. ——, 1923 "A lethal type in mice, which may live for a few days after birth " *Anat Rec* Vol 24, p 417.
41. De Witte, 1858 *Revue Numismatique*, Vol 3, pp 1-51
42. Dry, F W 1928 "The agouti coloration of the mouse (*Mus musculus*) and the rat (*Mus norvegicus*) " *Jour of Gen*, Vol 20, p 131
43. Dobrovolskaia-Zavadskaia, N 1929 ' Sur l'hérédité de la prédisposition au cancer spontané chez la souris ' *Cpt Rend Soc Biol*, Vol 101, pp 518-520
44. ——, 1927. "Brachyurie, accompaneé de condures et 'structure génétique' de la quéue chez la souris." *Cpt Rend Soc Biol*, Vol 97, pp 1583-1585

45 —— et N. Kobozieff, 1927 "Sur la reproduction des souris anoures." *Cpt. Rend. Soc. Biol.*, Vol 97, p. 116
46 Dunn, L C, 1916 "Genetic behavior of mice of the color varieties black-and-tan and red." *Amer. Nat.*, Vol 50, pp. 664–675
47. ——, 1920 "Sable varieties of mice." *Amer. Nat.*, Vol 54, pp 247–261
48 ——, 1920 "Independent genes in mice." *Gen.* Vol 5, pp 344–361.
49 ——, 1920 "Linkage in mice and rats." *Gen.*, Vol. 5, pp 325–343
50. ——, 1920 "Types of white spotting in mice." *Amer. Nat.*, Vol. 54, pp 465–495.
51 ——, 1928 "A fifth allelomorph in the agouti series of the house mouse." *Proc. Nat. Acad. Sci.*, Vol 14 pp 816–819
52. —— and Durham, G B, 1925 "The isolation of a pattern variety in piebald mice." *Amer. Nat.*, Vol 59, pp 36–49
53 Durham, F M, 1908 "Experiments on the coat color in mice" *Rep Evol Com Roy Soc*, Vol 4, pp 41–53
54. ——, 1911. "Further experiments on the inheritance of coat color in mice." *Jour. of Gen.*, Vol. 1, pp. 159–178.
55 Eversmann, 1848 "Mus wagneri." *Bull Soc. Imp Nat de Moscou*, Vol 21, pp 191–193
56 Farnell, L R, 1907 *Cults of the Greek States*, Vol 4, pp 164, 256
57 Feldman, H W, 1922. "A fourth allelomorph in the albino series in mice." *Amer. Nat.*, Vol 56, pp 573–574
58 ——, 1924 "Linkage of albino allelomorphs in rats and mice." *Gen.*, Vol 9, pp 487–492.
59 Fortuyn, von, A B D, 1912 "Ueber den systematischen wert der Japanischen Tanzmaus. (*Mus wagneri* var *rotans*, nov var.)" *Zool Anz*, Vol 39, pp 177–190
60 Gascoin, J S, 1856 "On a peculiar variety of *Mus musculus* (*Mus-nudoplicatus*)." *Proc Zool Soc*, London, Vol 24, pp 38–40
61 Gates, W H, 1925. "The Japanese waltzing mouse, origin and genetics." *Proc Nat Acad Sci*, Vol 11, p. 651
62 ——, 1927 "Linkage of short-ear and density in the house mouse." *Proc Nat Acad. Sci*, Vol 13, pp 575–578
63 ——, 1927. "A case of non-disjunction in the mouse." *Gen.*, Vol 12, pp. 295–306
64 ——, 1928 "Linkage of the factors for short-ear and density in the house mouse (*Mus musculus*)." *Gen.*, Vol 13, pp 170–179
65. Gesner, Conrad, 1551 *Historiæ Animalium* Zurich
66 Gordon, G, 1850 "Variety of the common or house mouse (*Mus musculus*)." *Zoologist*, Vol 8, pp 2763–2764
67. Guaita, von G, 1898. "Versuche mit Kreuzungen von verschiedenen Rassen der Hausmaus." *Berl. Nat Gesellsch.*, zu Freiburg, Vol 10, pp 317–332
68. ——, 1900 "Zweite Mittheilung ueber" etc *Berl. Nat Gesellsch.*, zu Freiburg, Vol. 11, pp. 131–138
69 Haacke, W, 1895 "Ueber Wesen, Ursachen und Verbung von Albinismus und Scheckung," etc, *Biol Centralblatt* No 15

70. HAACKE, W, 1906 "Die Gesetze der Rassenmachung und die Konstitution des Keimplasmas." *Arch Entw Mech*, No 21.
71. HAGEDOORN, A L, 1908 "Production of two varieties by one mutation in mice" *Cal Univ Pub in Phys*, Vol 3, p 87
72. ———, 1912 "The genetic factors in the development of the house mouse which influence coat color" *Zeit f Abst u rer*, Vol 6, pp 97-136
73. ———, 1914 "Repulsion in mice" (Reply) *Amer. Nat*, Vol 48, pp 699-700
74. HAHN, E, 1896 *Die Haustiere* Leipzig Duncker u Heimblot.
75. HALDANE, J. B S, et al 1915 "Reduplication in mice." *Jour of Gen.*, Vol. 5, pp. 133-135
76. HAMMERSCHLAG, V, 1912 "Zuchtversuche mit japanischen Tanzmauser u europaischen Laufmausen" *Arch Entw Mech*, Vol 33, pp 339-344
77. HEHN, V, 1911 *Kulturpflanzen und Haustiere* 8th Edition Berlin, Gebrüder Borntraeger
78. HUNT, H R and PERMAR, D, 1928 "Flexed tail, a mutation in the house mouse" *Anat Rec*, Vol 41, pp 117.
79. IBSEN, H L and STEIGLEDER, E, 1917 "Evidence for the death in utero of the homozygous yellow mouse" *Amer. Nat*, Vol. 51, pp 740-752
80. ILTIS, H, 1924 *Gregor Johann Mendel* Berlin, Julius Springer
81. JENKINSON, J W "A reinvestigation of the early stages of the development of the mouse." *Quart Jour. Micr Sci*, Vol 43, pp 61-82.
82. ———, 1911 "The development of the ear bones of the mouse." *Jour. Anat. and Physiol*, Vol 45, pp 305-318
83. JERINA. FRANCE, 1920 *Studien uber die Haararmut und Haarlosigkeit bei Haustieren* (Inaugural Dissertation) Univ Bern
84. JOHNSON, JOHN, 1640 *Historia Naturalis de Quadrupedibus* Francofurti, Matthai Meriani
85. KEELER, C E, 1924 "The inheritance of a retinal abnormality in white mice" *Proc. Nat. Acad Sci*, Vol 10, pp 329-333
86. ———, 1926 "On the occurrence in the house mouse of a Mendelizing structural defect of the retina producing blindness." *Proc Nat Acad Sci*, Vol 12, pp 255-258
87. ———, 1927. "Rodless retina, an ophthalmic mutation in the house mouse, *Mus musculus*" *Jour Exp Zool*, Vol 46, pp 355-407.
88. ———, 1927 "Le reflex irien à la lumière chez la souris a rétine sans bâtonnets." *Cpt. Rend Soc Biol*. Vol. 96, p 10
89. ———, 1927 "Iris movements in blind mice" *Amer Jour Physiol*, Vol 81, pp. 107-112
90. ———, 1927. "Absence héréditaire des bâtonnets chez la souris, *Mus musculus*" *Mem. Soc Zool. Fr*, Vol. 28, pp 48-60.
91. ———, 1927 "Sur l'origine du charactere 'sans bâtonnets' chez la souris domestique" *Bul Soc. Zool Fr*, Vol. 52, pp. 520-521.
92. ———, 1928. "The geotropic reaction of rodless mice in light and in darkness" *Jour. Gen Physiol*, Vol 11, pp 361-368.

93 ——, 1928 "The question of visual capacity in mice bearing rodless retinæ" *Zeitschr f. vergleich. Physiol*, Vol 7, pp 736-738

94 ——, 1928 "A description of the ontogenetic development of retinal action currents in the house mouse" *Proc Nat Acad Sci*, Vol 14, pp 811-815

95. ——, 1928 "Blind Mice" *Jour Exp. Zool*, Vol. 51, pp 495-508

96 ——, 1929 "The occurrence of a heritable twisted nose in the house mouse *Mus musculus*" *Proc Nat Acad Sci*, Vol 15, pp 838-839

97 ——, 1930 "'Parted frontals' in mice" *Jour. Hered.*, Vol 21, pp 19-20

98 ——, 1930 "Hereditary blindness in the house mouse with special reference to its linkage relationships" *Bull No 3, Howe Lab, Ophthal*, pp 1-11

99 KEELER, C E, SUTCLIFFE, EVELYN and CHAFFEE, E. L, 1928. "Normal and 'rodless' retinæ of the house mouse with respect to the electromotive force generated through stimulation by light." *Proc Nat Acad Sci*, Vol 14, pp 477-484

100 KELLER, OTTO, 1909 *Die Antike Tierwelt*. Leipzig, Wilhelm Englemann

101 KINGERY, H M, 1914 "So-called parthenogenesis in the white mouse" *Biol Bull*, Vol 27, pp 240-258

102 KINGSLEY J S, 1912 *Hertwig's Manual of Zoology* 3rd American Edition New York, Henry Holt & Co

103 KIRKHAM, W B, 1916 "The prolonged gestation period in suckling mice" *Anat Rec*, Vol 11, pp 31-40

104 ——, 1917 'Embryology of the yellow mouse' *Anat Rec*, Vol. 11, pp 480-481

105 ——, 1917 "The lethal factor in yellow mice" *Jour Gen*, Vol 8, p 217

106 ——, 1919 "The fate of homozygous yellow mice" *Jour Exp Zool*, Vol 28, pp 125-136

107 ——, 1920 "The life of the white mouse" *Proc Soc Exp Biol and Med*, Vol 17, pp 196-198.

108 LEBEDINSKY and DAUVART, 1927 "Atrichosis und ihre Vererbung bei der albinotischen Hausmaus" *Biol Centralbl*, Vol. 47, pp 748-752

109 LIPPINCOTT, W A, 1918 "The factors for yellow mice and notch in Drosophila" *Amer Nat*, Vol 52, pp 364-365.

110 LITTLE, C C, 1913. "Experimental studies in the inheritance of color in mice." *Carnegie Inst Wash Pub*, No 179

111. ——, 1914 "Dominant and recessive spotting in mice" *Amer. Nat*, Vol. 48, pp 74-82

112 ——, 1915 "Inheritance of black-eyed-white spotting in mice" *Amer Nat*, Vol 49, pp 727-740

113 ——, 1916 "The occurrence of three recognized color mutations in mice." *Amer Nat*, Vol 50, pp 335-349

114. ——, 1917. "Multiple factors in mice and rats" *Amer. Nat*, Vol 51, pp. 457-479.

115. LITTLE, C C , 1917 Relation of yellow coat color and black-eyed-white spotting of mice in inheritance." *Gen* , Vol 2, 433–444

116. ———, 1919 "A note on the fate of individuals homozygous for certain color factors in mice." *Amer Nat* , Vol 53, pp 185–187

117. ———, 1920. "Note on the occurrence of a probable sex-linked lethal factor in mammals." *Amer Nat* , Vol 54, pp 457–460

118. ———, 1920. "Is there linkage between the genes for yellow and for black in mice?" *Amer Nat* , Vol 54, pp 267–270

119. ———, 1920 "The heredity of susceptibility to a transplantable sarcoma (J W B) of the Japanese waltzing mouse." *Science*, Vol 51, pp 467–468

120. ——— and BAGG, H. J., 1924 "The occurrence of four inheritable morphological variations in mice and their possible relation to treatment with X-rays." *Jour Exp Zool* , Vol 41, pp 45–91

121. ——— and STRONG, L C , 1925 "Genetic studies on the transplantation of two adenocarcinomata." *Jour Exp Zool* , Vol 41, pp 93–114

122. ——— and TYZZER, E. E , 1916 "Further experimental studies on the inheritance of susceptibility to a transplantable tumor, carcinoma of the Japanese waltzing mice." *Jour Med Research*, Vol 33.

123. LOEB, L , 1921. "The inheritance of cancer in mice." *Amer Nat* , Vol 55, pp 510–528

124. ———, 1923 "The inheritance of cancer in mice." *Rept 2d Internat. Cong. Eug.*, Vol. 1, pp 182–183

125. LONG, J A and MARK, E L , 1911 "The maturation of the egg of the mouse." *Carnegie Inst Wash Pub* , No 142

126. LORD, E and GATES, W H , 1929 "Shaker, a new mutation of the house mouse." *Amer Nat* , Vol. 63, pp. 435–442

127. LYNCH, C J , 1921 "Short ears, an autosomal mutation in the house mouse." *Amer Nat* , Vol 55, pp 421–426

128. MACDOWELL, E C , ALLEN, EZRA and MACDOWELL, C G , 1929 "The relation of parity, age, and body weight to the number of corpora lutea in mice." *Anat Rec* , Vol 41, pp 267–272.

129. ———, "The prenatal growth of the mouse." *Jour Gen Physiol* , Vol 11, pp 57–70

130. MARSHALL, 1887 "Hairless mice in Humbolt Co.," *West Amer Science*, Vol 3, pp 72–73

131. MAYNARD, L A , 1930 "A diet for stock rats." *Science*, Vol 71, pp 192

132. MELISSINOS, K "Die Entwicklung des Eies der Mause." *Arch f Mikr Anat* , Vol 70, pp 577–628

133. MOORE, V A , 1916 *Pathology and Differential Diagnosis.* New York, Macmillan Co

134. MORGAN, T H , 1908 "Some experiments in heredity in mice." *Science*, Vol 27, p 493.

135. ———, 1909 "Recent experiments on the inheritance of coat color in mice." *Amer Nat* , Vol 43, pp 494–510

136 ———, 1911 "The influence of heredity and environment in determining the coat colors in mice." *Ann. N Y. Acad Sci*, Vol 21, pp 87-117

137 ———, 1914 "Multiple allelomorphs in mice" *Amer Nat*, Vol 48, pp 449-458

138 MOULTON, J HOPE, 1901 "Pestilence and mice" *Classical Review*, Vol 15, pp 284

139 MULLER, H J, 1927 "Artificial Transmutation of the Gene" *Science*, Vol 66, pp 84-87.

140 ONSLOW, H, 1915 "A contribution to our knowledge of the chemistry of coat color in animals and of dominant and recessive whiteness" *Proc Roy Soc*, London, Vol 89, pp 36-58

141 ———, 1917 "A note on certain names recently applied to sable mice." *Jour Gen*, Vol 6, pp 231-235

142 PAINTER, T S, 1927 "Chromosome constitution of Gates' 'nondisjunction' mice." *Gen*, Vol 12, pp 379-392

143 PALLAS, P S, 1766 *Zoographia Rosso-Asiatica* Petropoli, 1831

144 PARKES, A S, 1924 "Fertility in mice" *Brit Jour Exp Biol*, Vol 1924, pp 21-31

145 PEARSON, E S, 1924 'Congenital eye abnormalities in Albino Mice" *Nature*, Vol 114, p 433.

146 PINCUS, G, 1929 "A spontaneous mutation in the house mouse *Proc Nat Acad Sci.*, Vol. 15, pp 85-88

147 ———, 1929 "A mosaic (black-brown) coat pattern in the mouse" *Jour Exp Zool*, Vol 52, pp 439-441

148 PLATE, L, 1910 "Die Erbformeln der Farbenrassen von *Mus musculus*" *Zool Anz*, Vol 35, pp 634-640

149 ———, 1918 "Vererbungstudien an Mäusen" *Arch Entw Mech*, Vol 44, pp 291-336

150 PLINIUS, SECUNDUS C., 1635 *Historia Naturalis* (The historie of the world) London, Philemon Holland

151 POCOCK, R. I, 1904 Note bearing no title *Proc Zool Soc*, London, Vol 2, p 133

152 RABAUD, E, 1914. "Sur une anomalie héréditaire des membres posterieurs, chez la souris" *Cpt Rend Soc Biol*, Vol 77, pp 411-412

153 REINHARDT L, 1912 *Kulturgeschichte der Nutztiere* Munich, Ernst Reinhardt

154 RICHTER, M N and MACDOWELL, E C 1929. "The experimental transmission of leukemia in mice" *Proc Soc Biol Med*, Vol. 26, pp 362-364

155 SCHLUMBERGER, C, 1894 "Apropos d'un netsuké japonais" *Mem Soc. Zool de France*, Vol. 7, p. 63.

156 SCHOTT, CASPER, 1697 *Physica Curiosa* Herbipoli

157. SCHUSTER, E H J, 1905 "Results of crossing gray (house) mice with albinos" *Biometrika*, Vol 4, pp 1-12

158 SHARPE, R BOWDLER, 1908 'A guide to the domestic animals." *Brit Mus Nat. Hist.*

159. SNELL, G D, 1928 "A crossover between genes for short-ear and density in the house mouse." *Proc. Nat. Acad. Sci*, Vol 14, pp 926-928

160. ——, 1929 "Dwarf, a new Mendelian recessive character of the house mouse." *Proc Nat Acad Sci*, Vol 15, pp. 733-734.

161. ——, 1930. Unpublished (In press)

162. SO, M and IMAI, Y, 1919 "The types of spotting in mice and their genetic behavior" *Jour Gen*, Vol 9, pp 319-334

163. STRABO. Book XIII

164. STREATER, JOHN, 1667 *Pharmacopœia Londinensis* London

165. STRONG, L C, 1922 "A genetic analysis of the facts underlying susceptibility to transplantable tumors" *Jour Exp Zool*, Vol 36, pp 67-134

166. STURTEVANT, A. H, 1912 "Is there association between the yellow and agouti factors in mice?" *Amer Nat*, Vol 46. pp 368-371.

167. SUMNER, F. B, 1915. "Some studies of environmental influence, heredity, correlation and growth in the white mouse" *Jour Exp. Zool*, Vol 18, pp 325-432

168. ——, 1924 "Hairless mice" *Jour Hered*, Vol 15, pp 475-480

169. SWINDLER, M H, 1913 "Certain elements in the cults and ritual of Apollo" *Bryn Mawr College Monographs*, Vol XIII pp 1-77

170. TYZZER, E E, 1909 "A study of inheritance in mice with reference to their susceptibility to transplantable tumors" *Jour Med Research* Vol 21, pp 519-573

171. ——, 1928 (Collaborator) Section on pathological protozoa in Hans Zinsser's *A Textbook of Bacteriology* New York Appleton.

172. WACHTER, W L, 1921 "Data concerning linkage in mice" *Amer. Nat*, Vol 55, pp 412-420.

173. ——, 1927 "Linkage studies in mice" *Gen.*, Vol 12 pp 108-114.

174. WAUGH, K T, 1910 "The rôle of vision in the mental life of the mouse" *Jour Comp Neurol.*, Vol 20, pp 549-599

175. WEBSTER, L T, 1924 "Microbic virulence and host susceptibility in paratyphoid enteritis infection of white mice IV The effect of selective breeding in host resistance" *Jour Exp Med*, Vol 39, pp. 879-886.

176. WELDON, W. F R, 1903 "Mr Bateson's revision of Mendel's theory of heredity" *Biometrika*, Vol 2, pp 436-449

177. ——. 1907. "On heredity in mice from the records of the late W F R Weldon." *Biometrika*, Vol 5, pp 436-449.

178. ——, 1917 "Records of mice-breeding experiments.' *Biometrika*, Vol 11, Appendix pp 1-60

179. WERNEKE, F, 1916 "Die Pigmentierung der Farbenrassen von Mus musculus und ihre Beziehung zur Vererbung" *Arch. Entw Mech*, Vol. 42, pp 72-106

180. WHEELER, R 1912. "Feeding experiments with mice" *Jour Exp. Zool*, Vol 15, pp 209-223

181 WRIGHT, S , 1917 "Color inheritance in mammals" *Jour Hered* Vol 8, pp 224-233, 373-378
182 YERKES. R M , 1907 "The functions of the ear of the dancing mouse" *Amer Jour Physiol*, Vol 18 p xviii
183 ———, 1907 *The Dancing Mouse* The Macmillan Co , New York.
184 ZOTH, O , 1901 "Ein Beitrag zu den Beobachtungen und Versuchen an japanischen tanzmausen" *Arch f d. gesamte Physiol* , Vol 86, pp 147-176